Baedeker's

AA

Florence

THE AUTOMOBILE ASSOCIATION

Imprint

Cover picture: Cathedral of Santa Maria del Fiore

85 colour photographs
17 plans, 1 large city map

Conception and editorial work:
Redaktionsbüro Harenberg, Schwerte
English language: Alec Court

Text:
Linda and Heinz-Joachim Fischer, Rome

General direction:
Dr Peter Baumgarten, Baedeker Stuttgart
English translation: Babel Translations, Norwich

Cartography:
Ingenieurbüro für Kartographie Huber & Oberländer, Munich
Georg Schiffner, Lahr (city map)

Source of illustrations:
dpa (29), Historia-Photo (9), Italian State Tourist Office (22), Prenzel (2), Rogge (22),
ZEFA (1)

Following the tradition established by Karl Baedeker in 1844, sights of particular interest and hotels of outstanding quality are distinguished by either one or two asterisks.

To make it easier to locate the various sights listed in the "A to Z" section of the Guide, their coordinates on the large map of Florence are shown in red at the head of each entry.

Only a selection of hotels can be given: no reflection is implied, therefore, on establishments not included.

In a time of rapid change it is difficult to ensure that all information given is entirely accurate and up to date, and the possibility of error can never be entirely eliminated. Although the publishers can accept no responsibility for inaccuracies and omissions they are always grateful for corrections and suggestions for improvement.

© 1983 Baedeker Stuttgart
Original German edition

© 1983 Jarrold and Sons Ltd
English language edition worldwide

© The Automobile Association, 1983 57011
United Kingdom and Ireland

Reprinted 1985

Licensed user:
Mairs Geographischer Verlag GmbH & Co., Ostfildern-Kemnat bei Stuttgart

Reproductions:
Golz Repro-Service GmbH, Ludwigsburg

The name *Baedeker* is a registered trademark

Printed in Great Britain by Jarrold & Sons Ltd Norwich

ISBN 0 86145 183 X

AA/Baedeker:
Florence

Contents

Preface

This Pocket Guide to Florence is one of the new generation of Baedeker city guides.

Baedeker pocket guides, illustrated throughout in colour, are designed to meet the needs of the modern traveller. They are quick and easy to consult, with the principals sights described in alphabetical order and practical details about opening times, how to get there, etc., shown in the margin.

Each guide is divided into three parts. The first part gives a general account of the city, its history, population, culture and so on; in the second part the principal sights are described; and the third part contains a variety of practical information designed to help visitors to find their way about and make the most of their stay.

The new guides are abundantly illustrated and contain numbers of newly drawn plans. In a pocket at the back of the book is a large city map, and each entry in the main part of the guide gives the coordinates of the square on the map in which the particular feature can be located. Users of this guide, therefore will have no difficulty in finding what they want to see.

Facts and Figures

General

Florence is the main city of Tuscany, the central Italian region, and one of Italy's 20 "regioni". It is also the chief town of the Province of Florence.
Located on latitude 43°46'N and longitude 11°16'E, its altitude ranges from 160 ft (49 m) to 230 ft (70 m).

The city has 470,000 inhabitants and covers an area of 40 sq. miles (102 sq. km).
The Roman settlement of Florentia, which was established in 59 B.C., was almost square in shape. It stood on the right bank of the Arno and its northern border was on a line with where the Cathedral stands today, while the SW corner almost touched on the river. As the city boundaries gradually extended outwards under Byzantine rule in the 8th, 9th and 12th c. the left bank of the Arno also came to be part of the city. It was surrounded by a wall, sections of which can still be seen today.

Area and population

In the Middle Ages Florence was divided into four Quartieri (quarters), named after the city gates – San Piero, Duomo or Vescovo, San Pancragio and Santa Maria.
It was subsequently divided in six "Sestieri" (San Piero, Duomo, San Pancrazio, San Piero a Scheraggio, Borgo, Oltrano).
Nowadays Florence is divided into Quartieri, most of which are named after churches, including Santa Maria Novella, San Giovanni, Santa Croce, San Domenico and Santo Spirito. There are also the suburbs along the main trunk roads and on the hills of San Miniato, Belvedere and Bellosguardo in the S and Careggi, Montughi, Fiesole and Settignano in the N.

Districts

The Comune di Firenze are administered from the Palazzo Vecchio – which is the name chosen by the city authorities in preference to the more common Palazzo "della Signoria" or "Ducale". Communal elections are held every five years.
Subdivision into smaller adminstrative units is still in its early stages.

Administration

Population and Religion

The city's rise from the Colonia Florentia of the Roman veterans to the flourishing Florence of the Renaissance was a slow process. About 1300 the city had *c*. 30,000 inhabitants. By 1348 the number had risen to some 120,000 but only a third of the population survived the dreadful Plague of that year and the figure fell to 40,000.
The population figures did not reach 150,000 until the middle of the 19th c., since when they have continued to grow steadily.

Population

◄ *View of Florence and its Cathedral*

Religion

99% of the Florentines are Roman Catholic. The city is the seat of an Archbishop, whom the Pope traditionally elevates to the rank of Cardinal.
The city does have churches for other religious denominations as well as a synagogue.

Transport

Airport

Through Galileo Galilei Airport at Pisa, 53 miles (85 km) away, Florence has good national connections with other major Italian cities.
Peretola Airport in the immediate vicinity of the city is mainly for private and military purposes.

Rail and buses

Florence is an important junction for rail traffic in central Italy. All intercity trains converge on Santa Maria Novella, the main station.
Buses cater for local transport within the city.

Motorways and trunkroads

Florence was already an important trading post on the Via Cassia during the Roman Empire and it built upon its position in the Middle Ages. Today the city enjoys excellent commun-ications thanks to motorways, expressways and well-engineered trunk roads.
The city lies on the Autostrada del Sole, the motorway from Milan to Reggio di Calabria, and is also connected by motorway with Siena, Lucca, Pisa, Livorno and Genoa.
There are trunk roads to Bologna, Pontassieve (Forli and Arezzo), Siena, Empoli and Prato (Pistoia and Bologna).

Culture

Since the Renaissance Florence has retained its standing as a centre for art and culture. It has lost few of the churches and palaces, squares and bridges, frescoes and paintings which stem from the centuries when, in cultural terms, Florence was in its heyday. Since that time the city has been a magnet not only for tourists but also, and to an extraordinary degree, artists, art historians, and those engaged in restoration and historical sciences. Universities and institutes of scientific research, theatres and libraries, opera and concerts, all testify to the fact that the spirit of Florence lives on.

Universities and libraries

Florence has the following colleges: Università di Parigi, Università Europea, Università Internazionale dell'Arte, Uni-versità Libera per Attori.
Nine public libraries are at the disposal of scholars and the general public.

Academies and other agencies

With its buildings, churches, palaces and museums Florence offers unique opportunities for artistic and historical studies, which is why there are numerous academies (see Practical Information) and institutes concerned with science and culture. These include the Accademia della Crusca per la Lingua Italiana for the promotion of the Italian language, as well as various scientific institutes under the auspices of other nationalities.

People of Florence

Twelve theatres, headed by the Teatro Comunale, meet the demand for modern plays, classic drama and opera.
Florence has also won acclaim for its concerts, especially the offerings of the Maggio Musicale Fiorentina, the city's "musical month of May" which actually extends from the end of April until July.

Theatres and concerts

Commerce and Industry

International status

Since the Middle Ages the Florentines, as industrious craftsmen, astute businessmen and good civic administrators, have always made sure that they prosper. At a time when Florentine bankers dominated the European money market they influenced the course of European politics. The ruling family of Florence, the Medici, owed their rise to the success of their trading and banking enterprises.

After Florence failed to match the political power of the other Italian states – the Republic of Venice, Dukedom of Milan, the Vatican State and the Kingdom of Naples and Sicily – it lost its ranking in commercial terms and as a consequence today is not a prominent international centre for commerce or banking.

Traditional industries

Towards the end of the Middle Ages the Florentines owed their wealth to the textile industry (weaving, dyeing, garment making and the silk trade) and in its present form of the clothing industry this is still an important income sector. Its artistic traditions have been retained in the highly developed craft sector (earthenware, china, embroidery, leatherware and basketry). Most jobs are to be found in chemicals and pharmaceuticals, precision engineering, the antiques trade, printing and publishing.

Many of the agricultural products of Tuscany are also processed in Florence.

Service industries

The commercial sector is nowadays of the highest importance for the city. Innumerable banks have their head offices here, its fashion fairs ("Alta Moda") are world famous, and its furs and antiques attract visitors from home and abroad.

Also allied to this is the importance of tourism – there is a constant flow of visitors throughout the year and at holiday periods, especially at Christmas, Easter and during the summer, Florence is always full to capacity.

Since, as chief town for the Region of Tuscany and the Province of Florence, the city is also the seat of regional and local government, the services sector as a whole plays an important part in the city's economy.

Prominent Figures in Florentine History

Cosimo de' Medici the Elder was so impressed by the paintings of Fra Giovanni, a Dominican friar in the convent at Fiesole, that he brought him to the Florence convent of San Marco which the pious monk then adorned with a series of frescoes and panels, mostly as aids to contemplation, in the cells of the friars, depicting scenes from the lives of Christ, Mary and the saints. As a result San Marco became the world-famous museum that can be seen today. Fra Angelico's works attest to a profound faith; his gentle Madonnas are imbued with an almost supernatural radiance which is why, and possibly also because of his angel-like saintliness, he became known as "Fra Angelico" or "Beato Angelico". The principal colours of his paintings, red, blue and gold, conveying sublimity and holiness, are reminscent of medieval Gothic but his artistic forms anticipate the stylistic methods of the Renaissance. His grave is in Rome in the church of Santa Maria sopra Minerva.

Fra Angelico
(Fra Giovanni da Fiesole)
c. 1400–18.2.1455

The painter Botticelli, who spent virtually all his life in Florence and whose real name was Allessandro di Mariano Filipepi, is considered the foremost Florentine master of the early Renaissance. Most of his early works (Madonnas, portraits) were commissions for the Medici. He became famous mainly for his allegorical ("La Primavera" in the Uffizi), mythological ("Birth of Venus" in the Uffizi) and religious (Madonnas) portrayals of women. His pictures exhibit a fascinating sensuality which may be why he burnt some of his own paintings when urged to atone by the Dominican monk Girolamo Savonarola.
In 1480 Pope Sixtus IV summoned Botticelli to Rome where together with others he painted some of the frescoes for the walls of the Sistine Chapel.
Botticelli was also responsible for 94 pen and ink drawings in Dante's "Divine Comedy".

Sandro Botticelli
(Alessandro di Mariano
Filipepi)
1444/1445–17.5.1510

Filippo Brunelleschi, born in Florence, was the first Renaissance architect and one of the greatest. He was the first to evolve the laws of linear perspective and his adherence to a perspective framework is seen at its best in his greatest feat of architecture, the dome of the Cathedral of Santa Maria del Fiore. The most important buildings in Florence for which Brunelleschi was responsible are the Spedale degli Innocenti, the churches of San Lorenzo and Santo Spirito, and the Pazzi Chapel.
As a sculptor he entered his relief "The Sacrifice of Isaac" (1402–3) in the competition for the second bronze door of the Baptistery which was won by Ghiberti. Brunelleschi's entry can be seen today in the Museo Nazionale del Bargello.
His monument with a bust by Buggiano is in the Cathedral.

Filippo Brunelleschi
1377–1446

A true Renaissance figure of tremendous vitality and accomplishment, the Florentine sculptor and goldsmith Benvenuto Cellini made an impact on his contemporaries through the

Benvenuto Cellini
(3.11.1500–14.2.1571)

13

Sandro Botticelli

Filippo Brunelleschi

Cosimo I de' Medici

artistic merit of his work no less than through his adventurous life which he described in his famous biography.

In Florence his ability as a sculptor can be admired in his "Perseus with the Head of Medusa" (completed 1554) in the Loggia dei Lanzi and in the bust of Cosimo de' Medici in the Museo Nazionale del Bargello.

The most famous example of his work as a goldsmith, and probably the only one still extant, is the salt-cellar made for François I of France in the Museum of Art in Vienna.

Cimabue
(Giovanni Cenni di Pepo)
c. 1240–after 1302

Little is known of Cimabue, the "Father of Florentine Painting", whose real name was Giovanni Cenni di Pepo. He was active in Rome (1272) and in Pisa (1301–2), where he is thought to have been engaged on a very poorly preserved St John in the cathedral. At the end of the 13th c. he was working in Assisi (frescoes in the Upper Church of San Francesco) and Florence where the majestic and forceful Santa Trinità Madonna in the Uffizi is generally attributed to him. It is thought that he may well have been the teacher of Giotto and he was acclaimed by Dante as one of the most highly renowned painters of his time.

Cosimo il Vecchio
de' Medici
(Cosimo the Elder;
27.9.1389–1.8.1464)

Cosimo il Vecchio (i.e. Cosimo the Elder) was the first and the greatest of the Florentine Medici family to rule the city, serving the best interests of its citizens and contributing to the embellishment of Florence. Its people, inspired by ancient Rome, entitled him "Pater patriae", father of the fatherland. Jacopo da Pontormo's expressive posthumous painting of him in the Uffizi portrays Cosimo as an astute man, conscientious and musical, by no means handsome but with an engaging mentality.

The son of Giovanni Bicci, a successful banker and elected Gonfaloniere, Cosimo, together with his brother Giovanni, was already at the age of 31 acting on behalf of his family's diverse interests. He was banished in 1433 following one of the various power struggles among the noble families for the political reins of the city. He returned to Florence a year later, to the people's jubilation, and was elected Gonfaloniere, an office which he held until his death.

In addition to his political activities, Cosimo the Elder in his merchant capacity extended his banking business throughout

Europe. As a patron he was generous in his advancement of artists, entrusting the building of the Palazzo Medici to the architect Michelozzo, and transforming the convent of San Marco where he founded the library and set to work the painters Fra Angelico and Fra Filippo Lippi. He founded the collection in the Medici Library (Biblioteca Laurenziana) and the School of Philosophy where Marsilio Ficino taught.

Cosimo lived at the time of the Council of Florence (1439–43) which gave him an insight into ecclesiastical and European politics. At his death he left behind a well-ordered city state and was deeply mourned by its people.

It was thanks to Cosimo I, Duke of Florence from 1537 and Grand Duke of Tuscany, upon his appointment by Pope Pius IV, from 1569, that the Medici family regained a position of political power in Florence.

Cosimo I de' Medici
(11.6.1519–21.4.1574)

Cosimo's father, Giovanni delle Bande Nere – so called because of the black armour he wore at the head of his Black Bands of mounted soldiers – had squandered large sums of money with his constant military ventures. At 17 Cosimo made his entry into the political life of Florence and by tyrannical means brought the city under his rule. Once this was assured he set about revitalising its dormant economy and again made Florence a political power to be reckoned with.

As Duke of Florence he moved out of his family's townhouse, the Palazzo Medici, and into the Palazzo della Signoria which now became known as the Palazzo Ducale. Later he settled in the Palazzo Pitti, which became the political, artistic and intellectual hub of Florence, for Cosimo, a true Medici, was also patron to the artists of his time.

Successful though he may have been as a princely ruler, he did not enjoy the same measure of success in his private life. Seven of his eight children met with premature or cruel deaths.

Cosimo died in 1574, at the age of 55, after having handed over the affairs of state three years earlier to his son Francesco.

Dante Alighieri, Italy's greatest poet, was exiled from his native city.

Dante Alighieri
(May 1265–14.9.1321)

The son of a respected patrician family, Dante received his education from the Franciscans and Dominicans. He studied medieval philosophy, was interested in art and favoured a life of chivalry.

Florence was vouchsafed several years of peaceful prosperity after the reconciliation in 1279 of the warring Guelphs and Ghibellines, the parties of Pope and Emperor. When the hostilities recommenced Dante became embroiled on the side of the losing party which led to his banishment, on pain of death, from Florence. He was forced to live the rest of his life in exile and died in 1321 in Ravenna.

Yet Dante was haunted by two Florentine encounters. One of these was with Beatrice, the young girl he had known in childhood and whom, after her premature death, he passionately idealised in his poems; the other was with the city itself, at first loved by Dante and then hated and despised as "a city of shopkeepers". In his "Divine Comedy", the 3 by 33 cantos on Hell, Purgatory and Heaven, which came to be the prevailing concepts in the Western world of that time, Dante glorified Beatrice (thus ensuring her immortality) and passed judgement on the city of Florence and its citizens.

Prominent People in Florentine History

Donatello
(Donatello di Niccolò di Betto Bardi;
c. 1386–13.12.1466)

Not only the greatest Florentine sculptor before Michelangelo, Donatello also ranks as the most influential individual sculptor of the 15th c., unsurpassed by any other in terms of heroic expression, multiplicity of themes and range of creativity. Apprenticed to Ghiberti, he then worked with Nanni di Banco. In his native city of Florence he was responsible for sculpting statues on the façade, outer walls and Campanile of the Cathedral as well as for the church of Orsanmichele.

His study of the classical remains in Rome then led him far beyond the bounds of medieval artistic sensibilities and capacities. With his bronze David (c. 1430. in the Museo Nazionale del Bargello) he created the first free-standing nude of the Renaissance, the bronze Gattemalata monument in Padua is its first equestrian statue, and Judith and Holofernes (1440), inside the Palazzo Vecchio, its first free-standing monumental group. Also outstanding are the Tabernacle with the Annunciation (c. 1434) in the church of Santa Croce and the Cantoria with dancing children for the Cathedral (1433–40, in the Museo dell'Opera del Duomo). His carved wooden Magdalene for the Baptistery (c. 1455, now also in the Cathedral Museum) exemplifies his ability as a sculptor to match beauty with ugliness and was crucial in the development of Florentine painting. The Medici honoured the sculptor by assenting to his interment in the crypt of Cosimo il Vecchio in San Lorenzo.

Lorenzo Ghiberti
(1378–1.12.1455)

Lorenzo Ghiberti achieved undying fame through the two bronze doors which he made for the Baptistery (Battistero San Giovanni) in Florence. It was as a painter that he entered the competition for the North Door, which he won. He devoted 21 year's work, from 1403 to 1424, to these doors but his greatest masterpiece was to be the East pair of doors, the "Porta del Paradiso", which he rightly inscribed "mira arte fabricatum" – "made with admirable art".

The scenes on the doors from the Old and New Testament, framed by saints, fathers of the Church and ornamentation, display Ghiberti's expressive capability as an artist, and his technical craft as a sculptor. Distinguished by their harmony of form and balance of movement, they signify his ability to link the Gothic expression of piety with the antique ideal of beauty of the Renaissance.

His three figures for the church of Orsanmichele are the first large bronzes of the new era in art.

Ghiberti was also an architect (collaboration on Florence Cathedral), goldsmith (unfortunately no work extant) and author (commentaries on Italian art of the 13th c., including his Autobiography).

In his workshops Ghiberti also employed other artists, including Michelozzo and Donatello.

Ghirlandaio
(Domenico di Tommaso Bigordi;
1449–11.1.1494)

Although Ghirlandaio's principal claim to fame is that Michelangelo Buonarroti was his apprentice, he was also the best fresco executant of his generation in Florence and responsible for typical examples of renaissance art: lively groups of his fellow Florentines against a landscape or an architectural background in confident perspective.

Ghirlandaio's principal works are six frescoes in the church of Santa Trinità, depicting scenes from the life of St Francis (1485) and frescoes of the lives of Mary and John the Baptist in the choir of Santa Maria Novella.

Dante Alighieri

Leonardo da Vinci

Lorenzo de' Medici

In his later paintings the collaboration of his pupils becomes progressively more evident.

The most famous sculptor in Florence after the death of Michelangelo, Giovanni da Bologna, known in Italy as Giambologna, was born in Flanders. He came to Italy in 1550, first to Rome then to Florence where he chose to settle and entered the service of the Medici in 1556.

Giovanni da Bologna (Giambologna; 1529–13.8.1608)

In 1579 this original and adventurous artist wrote to Ottavio Farnese that he was not so much concerned with the content of his work as with constantly testing his ability to shape a figure or a group with the greatest possible ingenuity and intensity of expression.

His sculptures in bronze and marble can be seen at many sites in Florence: the Piazza della Signoria (equestrian statue of Cosimo I de' Medici), in the convent of San Marco (reclining bronze figure in the Sacristy), in the Palazzio Vecchio, in the Loggia dei Lanzi (Rape of the Sabines), in the Giardino di Boboli of the Palazzo Pitti (statue of Abundance) and in the Museo Nazionale del Bargello (inter alia "Winged Mercury").

The name of Giotto di Bondone as architect is inexorably linked with the Campanile, the belfry of Florence Cathedral (Duomo Santa Maria del Fiore).

Giotto di Bondone (c. 1266–8.1.1337)

As an artist Giotto, together with Cimabue, is generally regarded as the founder of modern painting since, also influenced by French Gothic, he broke away from dependence on the stereotyped formality of Byzantine iconography.

Giotto's style of painting is based directly on the principle of direct observation of nature and reality, achieving a fresh approach to the stories of the Bible and the legends of the saints. His frescoes in the church of Santa Croce of scenes from the lives of St John the Baptist, St John the Evangelist and St Francis, his Ognissanti Madonna in the Uffizi and the frescoes in the Arena Chapel, Padua, are world-famous.

The Italian Renaissance brought a host of versatile personalities to the fore but it was only the genius of Leonardo da Vinci that brought together the skills of painter, sculptor, architect, natural scientist and engineer. He was comparable only with Michelangelo (they disliked one another intensely!) He was

Leonardo da Vinci (15.4.1452–2.5.1519)

17

the consummate artist of the Renaissance; his findings and research in the technical sphere demonstrate his universality of spirit.

Leonardo da Vinci was a pupil of Verrocchio and in 1472, at the age of 20, was already a Master in the Florentine Guild of Painters (first large-scale work of his own "Adoration of the Magi" in the Uffizi). From 1482 to 1498 he worked at the court of Duke Lodovico Sforza in Milan ("Virgin of the Rocks" and "Last Supper" in the refectory of the convent of Santa Maria delle Grazie, badly damaged). He worked in Florence again from 1500 to 1506, then in Milan and finally, from 1513 to 1516, in Rome. In 1517 he moved to France at the invitation of King François I.

The work carried out in the last twenty years of his life has almost all been lost or survives only in the form of copies by his pupils. The "Mona Lisa", probably his most famous painting, is in the Louvre in Paris, together with "Madonna and Child with St Anne". He started a wall-painting of the Battle of Anghiari for the Palazzo Vecchio in Florence but all but a section of the cartoon has been lost and nothing remains of the painting. The original scale model for a bronze equestrian monument of Duke Francesco Sforza was destroyed.

Leonardo was the architect of fortresses, devoted himself to intensely scientific projects, dissected corpses, wrote and illustrated an essay on the anatomy of the human body, projected aircraft and helicopters, made observations on the flight of birds, investigated the laws governing the movement of air and water and conducted botanical and geological studies. His many drawings, studies of movement in the human body, research into natural science, designs for buildings and technical projects attest to the catholicity of this Renaissance genius.

Lorenzo de' Medici
(Lorenzo the Magnificent;
1.1.1449–8.4.1492)

Lorenzo de' Medici, was a typical Renaissance prince in his attitudes, education, patronage and style of government. ·
Lorenzo made use of the Medici banking funds and the backing of the people of Florence to raise the city to a position of cultural and political prominence in Italy. His brother Giuliano fell victim to the Pazzi conspiracy in the Cathedral in 1478 when Lorenzo, wounded, managed to take refuge in the sacristy. After the Pazzi affair the constitution was changed so that power was concentrated in his hands. A patron of the Platonic Academy, he was himself a talented poet. In the Medici Garden near San Marco he assembled a collection of Classical sculpture, brought the sculptors of his time together and was responsible for talented young men such as Michelangelo getting their training. Work was carried out on his behalf by Andrea del Verrocchio (Putto and Dolphin in the Cortile of the Palazzo Vecchio), Ghirlandaio and Sandro Botticelli. When Lorenzo died from a mysterious illness at the age of 43 Niccolò Machiavelli wrote: "Never perished in Italy a man famed for such great astuteness nor was a man's death such a great sorrow for his fatherland. Every fellow citizen mourns his death, not one forebore to manifest his grief at this event."

Lorenzo was originally interred in the old sacristy of San Lorenzo then subsequently laid to rest with his brother in the new sacristy designed by Michelangelo.

Niccolò Machiavelli

Michelangelo Buonarroti

Raphael

Niccolò Machiavelli, the great chronicler of Florentine history, is also the much maligned philosopher of man's struggle for power.

Niccolò Machiavelli
(3.5.1469–22.6.1527)

After the Medici were driven out of Florence in 1494 Machiavelli was secretary to the executive Council of Ten and therefore directly involved in the government of the Republic. He was often employed as an envoy on missions abroad. The Medici returned in 1512 and resumed power in Florence. From that time onwards Machiavelli withdrew to dedicate himself to literary pursuits, a watchful and astute observer of the political scene.

His major works are his discourses on the first ten books of Livy in which he expounds, through examples from Roman history, his ideas about the power of the State and the vicissitudes of history, and his most famous work "Il Principe", "The Prince", which he completed in 1513 (not published until 1532) and in which he elaborated the political doctrine, the "Machiavellism" that entered into Western political thought, that the end justifies the means, however reprehensible, if it is for the good of the State.

Michelangelo Buonarroti, painter, sculptor, architect and poet, brought the art of the Renaissance to the peak of perfection.

Michelangelo Buonarroti
(6.3.1475–18.2.1564)

In 1488, at the age of 13, Michelangelo was apprenticed to the Florentine painter Domenico Ghirlandaio. Besides his aptitude for painting he increasingly developed his passionate interest in sculpture. In 1489 the young Michelangelo transferred to the school for sculptors set up in the Medici Garden. He left Florence in 1494 (before the expulsion of the Medici and the ensuing political upheaval when the Dominican monk Savanarola seized power) and, after a brief sojourn in Venice, worked in Bologna. He returned to Florence (1495–6) then journeyed to Rome where he stayed from 1496 until 1501. His "Bacchus" (Museo Nazionale del Bargello) and the Pietà for St Peter's in Rome date from this period.

Michelangelo was back in Florence from 1501 to 1505, when he created his "David" (Galleria dell'Accademia), the Bruges Madonna, the "Madonna Pitti" tondo (Bargello) and the painting "The Holy Family" (Galleria degli Uffizi). Because of his restless spirit, the years between 1505 and 1534 were spent wandering between Florence, Rome and Bologna to work on commissions. During these years his achievements included the frescoes on the ceiling of the Sistine Chapel in the Vatican, the funerary chapel for the Medici in San Lorenzo in Florence, "Moses" for the tomb of Julius in Rome, the Boboli Slaves (Accademia), "Apollo" (Bargello) and "Vittoria" (Palazzo Vecchio). From 1534 until his death in 1564, apart from brief interludes, Michelangelo lived in Rome ("Last Judgement" on the altar wall of the Sistine Chapel in the Vatican, bust of Brutus in the Bargello, figures for the tomb of Julius in Rome, Projects for the Biblioteca Laurenziana at San Marco in Florence, and, in Rome, the Piazza del Campidoglio and, his greatest architectural achievement, the dome of St Peter's). The work of his old age, the marble group of the Pietà in Florence Cathedral (Opera del Duomo) and a few lines of his verse manifest the suffering of this great artist:

"Released of the burden that I groaning bore,
At last set free from all earthly desires,
A frail barque, to Thee, O Lord, I steer my course
From storm-tossed seas to Thy calm still waters."

Michelangelo's body was brought from Rome and laid to rest in the church of Santa Croce.

Raphael
(Raffaello Santi;
1483–6.4.1520)

Raphael, whose real name was Raffaello Santi or Sanzio, was the artist whose paintings most clearly and comprehensively represented the High Renaissance at its apogee, especially his Madonnas and his frescoes for the Vatican "The School of Athens" and the "Disputa".

Born in Urbino, the son of the painter Giovanni Santi, he became a pupil of Perugino in Perugia at the age of 17. In 1504 he moved to Florence where he set about learning all he could from the works of past and contemporary artists. After 1508 he lived in Rome where he succeeded Bramante (d. 1514) as architect of the new St Peter's. His twelve years in Rome were marked by his greatest artistic achievement, the Stanze de Raffaello frescoes in the Vatican.

Raphael's numerous paintings to be seen in Florence include: Pope Leo X with two Cardinals, Pope Julius II, Madonna with the Goldfinch and Portrait of Perugino in the Uffizi (Galleria degli Uffizi) and La Donna Velata, La Donna Gravida, Madonna del Granduca, Madonna della seggiola, Baldachin Madonna and Madonna dell'impannata in the Palazzo Pitti.

Raphael died at the age of 37 and was the only artist to be accorded the honour of burial in the Pantheon in Rome.

History of Florence

The Romans found Florentia near the former Etruscan settlement of Fiesole.	*c.* 300 B.C.
Florentia becomes a veterans colony under Julius Caesar.	59 B.C.
The Ostrogoths under Radagasius lay siege to Florence but are beaten off by Stilicho.	A.D. 406
The Byzantine General Belisarius defeats the Ostrogoths under Totila.	539–41
The Lombards rule Northern Italy which is nominally part of the Eastern Roman Empire. They found the Duchy of Tuscia.	from 568
Charlemagne overthrows Desiderius, the Lombard King, and makes Tuscia a Frankish Margraviate.	774
Gerhard, a Cluniac reformer, becomes Bishop of Florence.	1045
Gerhard of Florence is installed as Pope Nicholas II.	1059
Matilda, Countess of Tuscia, mediates at Canossa in the investiture dispute between Emperor Henry IV and Pope Gregory VII.	1077
Matilda abandons her role as mediator in the investiture dispute and wills her estates other than Florence, Lucca and Siena (i.e. the Matildan inheritance) to the Pope. Florence through siding with Matilda becomes one of the main allies of the Pope in the struggle against non-clerical influences.	*c.* 1079
Matilda grants Florence autonomous rights as a city.	1115
Florence destroys its neighbouring rival city Fiesole.	1125
Under the rule of the nobility Florence has risen to the position of the leading power in Tuscany.	*c.* 1200
Emperor Frederick II conquers the Lombard league and the Pope excommunicates him. Frequent manifestations of the antagonism between the Ghibellines, the party of the Empire, and the Guelphs, the faction of the Church.	1237
The first Council of Lyons declares that Frederick II is deposed. Besides the factional disputes of the Guelphs and the Ghibellines Florence is riven by serious social strife between the nobility and the guilds of merchants and craftsmen.	1245
The Guelphs flee from the city.	1248
The Guelphs win the upper hand prior to the death of Frederick II. The imperial officials are dismissed and the guilds promulgate their own constitution, ushering in the era of "il Primo Popolo", the First Democracy.	1250

History of Florence

1252	Florence begins minting a gold ducat called the Fiorino or Florenus. This becomes current throughout Europe (hence the name "florin" for the Dutch guilder and the two-shilling coin in Britain).
1255	The Palazzo Pubblico is built to house the city's first democratic government.
1282	The new democratic constitution strengthens the "greater guilds" (arti maggiori) of the merchants against the "lesser guilds" (arti miniori) of the artisans.
1284	The third city wall is built to form an encircling defensive system but serves mainly to demonstrate political power.
1293	The Gonfaloniere (banner-bearer of Justice) replaces the Podestà (executive) and is meant to safeguard the interests of the commoners against the nobility. The chief authority is the Signoria under the direction of the Gonfaloniere.
1294	Start of building work on the Cathedral Santa Maria del Fiore.
1299	Building of the Palazzo Vecchio.
1302	The Guelphs banish the Ghibellines (including Dante) from Florence.
1333	The Arno floods and destroys many bridges and buildings.
1334	Pope Benedict XIII forbids the use of the names Ghibelline and Guelph under pain of banishment.
1340	First great Plague.
1347–8	Famine and a second plague epidemic reduce the Florentine population by one third.
1348	Vieri de Cambio de' Medici founds the first historically recorded Medici Bank.
1378	The revolt of the "Ciompi", an uprising led by the woolworkers, briefly achieves greater democratisation.
from 1405	Through the purchase (1405) and subjection (1406) of Pisa Florence achieves greater supremacy in Tuscany. The city is governed by an oligarchic junta headed by the Albizzi family.
1421	Florence gains access to the sea by acquiring the ports of Livorno and Portopisano and secures a prominent position in European trade. Giovanni di Bicci de' Medici becomes Gonfaloniere.
1433	Following defeat in the war against Lucca the Albizzi-dominated oligarchy place Cosimo the Elder under arrest and have him sentenced to ten years' banishment from the city.
1434	Rinaldo degli Albizzi falls from office and Cosimo de' Medici is recalled from exile to take his place as Gonfaloniere.
1439	The 17th Council meets in Florence.

Cosimo the Elder commissions the Palazzo Medici and founds the Medici Library (now Biblioteca Laurenziana).

1444

Florence enjoys its greatest prosperity under Lorenzo the Magnificent (il Magnifico). The Medici Bank is weakened by mismanagement and lack of co-ordination.

1469–92

Two members of the Pazzi banking family, backed by Pope Sixtus IV, make an attempt on the lives of Giuliano and Lorenzo de' Medici. Lorenzo is wounded but survives. The conspirators are hanged. The constitution of Florence is redrafted on monarchic lines.

1478

The Dominican Friar and revivalist preacher Girolamo Savonarola calls on Florence to repent, announces the imminence of the Last Judgement and calls for reform of the Church.

1482

Savonarola elevates the convent of San Marco to a monastic congregation in its own right with a strict ascetic rule.

1493

Charles VIII of France invades Italy. Piero de' Medici, without consulting the Signoria, surrenders to him at Pisa. The Medici are driven out of Florence.
Savonarola declares Christ the King of Florence and establishes a theocracy with statutes based on the Gospels.

1494

Savonarola is tortured then publicly executed by hanging and burning.

1498

As Gonfaloniere Piero Soderini carries out reforms and recaptures rebellious Pisa.

1502–12

Return of the Medici.

1512

Second expulsion of the Medici.

1527

Emperor Charles V makes the Medici hereditary Dukes of Florence.

1531

Conquest of Siena.

1559

Grand Duchy of Tuscany with Florence as chief town.

from 1569

Death of the last Medici. The Grand Duchy passes to the Austrian House of Lorraine.

1737

The city enjoys a fresh period of prosperity as provisional capital of the new Kingdom of Italy.

1865–70

Republic of Italy.

1946

Florence suffers disastrous floods when the Arno bursts its banks. Countless dead and homeless and considerable damage to the historic fabric and art treasures of the city.

1966

Quotations

Leondro Alberti
(1568)

"The city is very fair and rightly bears the name of Florence the Fair, the flower of Italy. There one sees magnificent buildings, some dedicated to God, some for the use of its citizens. One's gaze first falls upon the wondrous temple of Santa Maria del Fiore, all clad with marble, with the sublime cupola created by that most excellent Florentine, the architect Brunelleschi."

Jacob Burckhardt
(25.5.1818–8.8.1897)
Swiss art historian

"One finds united in the history of Florence the highest degree of political awareness and the greatest wealth of cultural forms, and in this sense the city may well have earned the title of the world's first modern state. Here it is an entire populace that engages in what is in the princely states a family affair. The wonderful Florentine spirit, at the same time artistic and acutely reasoning, unremittingly reshapes the political and social condition and describes and judges that same condition just as unremittingly. Thus Florence became the home of political doctrines and theories, of experiments and advances, but together with Venice the home of statistics and solely and above all other states in the world the home of historical image-making in the modern sense."

Cosmino the Elder
(Cosimo il Vecchio)
27.9.1389–1.8.1464

Guilding principle:
"Kingdoms fall through extravagance,
Cities rise through being austere.
See the Haughty, struck down by unseen hand."

Charles Dickens
(7.2.1812–9.6.1870)
English author
"Pictures from Italy"

"How much beauty is here, when, on a fair clear morning, we look, from the summit of a hill, on Florence! See where it lies before us in a sun-lighted valley, bright with the winding Arno, and shut in by swelling hills; its domes, and towers, and palaces, rising from the rich country in a glittering heap, and shining in the sun like gold!
Magnificently stern and sombre are the streets of beautiful Florence; and the strong old piles of building make such heaps of shadow, on the ground and in the river, that there is another and a different city of rich forms and fancies, always lying at our feet."

Max Frisch
(b.15.5.1911)
Swiss author

"In the chamber of Savonarola: the man is fascinating, the profile, next to it the small picture of his funeral pyre, the black face of the right-thinking, yet one must allow these judges something: they will soon be witnessing the execution, everything is ready on time, in its place, a wooden walkway leads from the court to the red flames. Here I sense something akin to my recent feelings at the Fishmarket: all the circumstances are public, on view in a human dimension, not anonymous."

"Florence is a manly town, and the cities of art that appeal to the current sensibility are feminine, like Venice and Siena. What irritates the modern tourist about Florence is that it makes no concession to the pleasure principle. It stands four-square and direct, with no air of mystery, no blandishments, no furbelows – no Gothic lace or baroque swirls . . . The great sculptors and architects who stamped the outward city with its permanent image or style – Brunelleschi, Donatello, Michelangelo – were all bachelors. Monks, soldier-saints, prophets, hermits were the city's heroes. Saint John the Baptist, in his shaggy skins, feeding on locusts and honey, is the patron, and, except for the Madonna with her baby boy, women saints count for little in the Florentine iconography."

Mary McCarthy
(b.21.6.1912)
American writer "The Stones of Florence"

"The Italians say 'Firenze'. Compared with the English and French 'Florence' this has a hard, almost harsh sound. That is why d'Annunzio wanted people to use the old name, Fiorenza, which is what Dante called his native city. D'Annunzio's suggestion was not taken up, however. The sober, austere Florentines found the old name too rich, and, to a certain degree, too extravagant."

Eckart Peterich
(16.12.1900–13.4.1968)
German author

"The Cathedral, together with Campanile and Baptistery, is the most magnificent building in the city and I first turned my step in its direction after I had gazed my fill upon the Piazza del Gran Duca with its impressive Loggia dei Lanzi and many colossal statues, including those by Giovanni da Bologna of which I had become particularly fond. The Campanile adorned with fine multi-coloured marble exerts an immediate charm and surpasses in reality any image of it that I have ever seen. It is clear from the very first glimpse that its creator was an artist rather than a builder for it is colour that predominates among the elements brought together to such charming effect."

Max Nohl
Italian Sketchbook
(1805)

"Apart from some Dutch cities, Florence is probably the cleanest city in the world and certainly one of the most elegant. Its neo-Gothic architecture possesses all the purity and perfection of a lovely miniature. Fortunately for the beauty of the city, its citizens, when they lost their freedom, also lost the energy to embark on large buildings. In consequence nowhere here is the eye affronted by an ignoble façade and there is nothing to disturb the fair harmony of these streets which are imbued with the medieval ideal of beauty."

Stendhal
(23.1.1783–23.3.1842)
French writer

Florence from A to Z

Academy

See Galleria dell'Accademia

Arciconfraternità della Misericordia   J5
("Archconfraternity of Mercy")

This Order, the oldest and most distinguished association of Florentine citizens for social and charitable purposes, was founded in 1326, when the Plague raged in Florence, to aid the sick poor and attend to their burial. Michelangelo was a member of the Order which used to wear red hoods (these are now black) and which has its headquarters near the Duomo Santa Maria del Fiore (see entry). The duties of the Order used to include accompanying condemned prisoners to the place of execution. Nowadays the confraternity runs a modern ambulance service and a first-aid centre. It has over 2000 members, all volunteers, and is funded by donations.

Location
Piazza del Duomo 19

Buses
B, 1, 4, 6, 7, 10, 11, 13r, 14, 17, 19r, 23, 25, 31, 32, 33

Arcispedale di Santa Maria Nuova (Hospital)   K5

Early in the 14th c. Florence's old hospital was considerably enlarged and renamed Santa Maria Nuova (St Mary the New). Most of the present spacious building between Via degli Alfani, Via della Pergola, Via Bufalini and Via Sant'Egidio dates from the 17th c. An interesting feature is the clearcut articulation of the loggias overlooking Piazza Santa Maria Nuova.

Location
Piazza di Santa Maria Nuova

Buses
13r, 14, 19r, 23, 31, 32, 33

*Badia Fiorentina (Church)   K6

The spire of the Badia opposite the Palazzo del Bargello (see entry) is an unmistakable feature of the skyline of Florence. This church of a Benedictine abbey was founded in 978 by Willa, the mother of Ugo, Margrave of Tuscany (commemorated here every year on 21 December, the anniversary of his death). The church was subsequently enlarged by Arnolfo di Cambio in the 13th c. and then internally virtually rebuilt in the Baroque style by Matteo Segaloni in the 17th c.
Interesting features of the Gothic façade are the portal by Benedetto da Rovezzano (1495) with a "Madonna and Child" (early 16th c.) in glazed terracotta by Benedetto Buglioni in the lunette.
A walk round the church should take in the following points of interest:

Location
Via del Proconsolo
(access from Via Dante Alighieri also)

Buses
13, 14, 19, 23, 31, 32

◀ *Badia Fiorentina and its distinctive church spire*

Filippino Lippi's masterpiece (1485) "The Madonna appearing to St. Bernard" (left of the entrance).
Tomb of Ugo, Margrave of Tuscany (d. 1001), built between 1469 and 1481 by Mino da Fiesole (in the left transept).
The beautiful 15th c. cloister, popularly known as the "Chiostro degli Aranci" because of its orange trees.

Battistero San Giovanni (Baptistery)   J5

Location
Piazza S. Giovanni

Buses
B, 1, 4, 6, 7, 10, 11, 14, 17, 19, 23, 25, 31, 32

The "Baptistery of St John" or, in Dante's words, "il bel San Giovanni", was completed about 1128, 70 years after building had commenced. It is famous for the three massive bronze doors on the S, N, and E sides and for the magnificent mosaics in its octagonal interior.
A number of builders were responsible for the construction of what, after 1128, was to serve as a baptistery. Its pleasing proportions and green and white marble scheme of decoration made it an architectural masterpiece that was to serve as a model for other European buildings. The three bronze portals – works of sculpture unsurpassed in the Western world – were added in the 15th c.

S portal

The S portal is the oldest and was designed by Andrea Pisano (1318–30) and cast by Leonardo d'Avanzano (1330–8). It is divided into 28 square Gothic panels. With workmanship reminiscent of the art of the goldsmith, the reliefs on 20 of the panels depict scenes from the life of John the Baptist, patron saint of the church; the other eight panels are allegorical representations of the theological and cardinal virtues. Every figure stands out in clear relief, each one a unique work of art in the modelling of the face, of the folds of the garments and the expressive posture of the body.
The decorations of the framing are by Vittorio Ghiberti, son of Lorenzo, and their foliage, creatures and fruit are an early indication of the wealth of form that characterised the Renaissance.

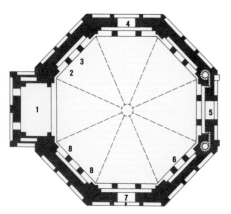

Battistero San Giovanni

1 Tribuna (high altar) with mosaics by Jacopo

2 Sarcophagus of Bishop Ranieri

3 Tomb of the Antipope John XXIII

4 N door

5 E door (Porta del Paradiso)

6 Marble font

7 S door (entrance)

8 Roman sarcophagi

In 1401 Lorenzo Ghiberti beat six others (including Brunelle-schi and Jacopo della Quercia) to win the competition for the N portal. From 1403 to 1424 Ghiberti worked on the bronze doors with his assistants (Masolino, Donatello, Paolo Uccello, Bernardo Ciuffagni, Bernardo Cennini) and in doing so adhered closely to Andrea Pisano's design for the S portal: 28 square panels each with a Gothic relief, twenty of them scenes of the Life of Christ and eight of them the figures of the four Evangelists and four Early Fathers of the Latin Church. His work, however, far excels that of Pisano in the grace of the figures and the liveliness of expression. Ghiberti's difference of approach, while still keeping to the traditional forms, is particularly evident in the vivid scenes of the "Resurrection" (right-hand door, top row, left), the "Baptism" and the "Temptation of Jesus" (left-hand door, 4th row down, left and right), the "Nativity" (left-hand door, 5th row down, right) and "Christ among the Doctors" (right-hand door, 5th row down, right).

Ghiberti also designed the bronze framing of the portal from which small heads protrude at every intersection.

Ghiberti adopted an entirely new approach when he came to design his greatest work, the E portal. Michelangelo considered it worthy to serve as the Gate of Paradise (hence the name "Porta del Paradiso") and Ghiberti himself sang its praises by adding "mira arte fabricatum" ("made with admirable art") on the right-hand door next to his signature.

N portal

E portal

N door　　　　*S door*　　　　*E door*

Battistero San Giovanni

Nowhere else has a sculptor expressed himself in bronze as perfectly as in this door, created between 1425 and 1452. The ten separate panels contain reliefs of scriptural subjects. The framing incorporates figures of prophets and sibyls and portrait medallions, including one of Ghiberti himself (4th from the top in the middle row on the left).

The beauty and mastery of the finely delineated perspectives, the three-dimensional levels of representation, the individual characterisation of the figures, the meaningful composition of the groupings, all combine in the consummate perfection of the whole.

From top left to bottom right the panels depict the following:
Adam and Eve: creation, fall, expulsion from the Garden.
Cain and Abel: sacrifice of Cain and Abel, death of Abel, punishment of Cain.
Noah: his sacrifice, departure from the Ark, his drunkenness.
Abraham and Isaac: angel appearing to Abraham, Isaac's sacrifice.
Jacob and Esau: birth of Esau and Jacob, selling the birthright, Esau hunting, Rebecca, Isaac's betrayal.
Joseph: selling of Joseph, Benjamin, Joseph and his brothers.
Moses: Moses receiving the Tablets of the Law on Mount Sinai.
Joshua: the Jews before Jericho, encampment, the walls come tumbling down at the sound of the trumpets.
Saul and David: Saul in battle against the Philistines, slaying of Goliath.
Solomon and the Queen of Sheba.
This door rightly has the place of honour opposite the Duomo Santa Maria del Fiore (see entry).

Porta del Paradiso: Moses receiving the Tablets of the Law on Mount Sinai

The sombre, mystical nature of the dim interior of the Baptistery comes as something of a surprise after the clearcut articulation of the exterior. It is dominated by the octagonal dome (diameter 84 ft – 25·6 m) which is completely lined with mosaics, the work of Florentine artists (Jacopo da Torrita, Cimabue, Andrea di Riccio, Gaddo Gaddi) in the 13th c. or possibly about 1300 and therefore at the time of Dante. One of the greatest mosaics in the Western world, it is as outstanding for its treatment of its subject matter as for the richness of its ornamentation.

Interior

In the centre is the gigantic figure of Christ as Judge of the World at the Last Judgement. Grouped around him, in different sections, are the figures of the Resurrected and the Damned, of angels, apostles, prophets and saints, with Mary and John the Baptist ranged against the realm of the Devil, devourer of men. (It should be recalled that Dante, Italy's greatest poet, who in his "Divine Comedy" describes Heaven, Purgatory and Hell, came from Florence.) Other vivid mosaics depict the "Creation of the World", scenes from the life of Joseph and of Jesus Christ, Mary and John the Baptist.

Also of interest are one of Donatello's masterpieces, the tomb of the Antipope John XXIII (deposed by the Council of Constance) and the niello decoration of the marble floor (zodiac and ornamentation), the marble font, the sarcophagus of Bishop Ranieri and the high altar with a candlestick in the form of an angel.

Another of Donatello's masterpieces used to stand in the Baptistery – his wooden statue of Mary Magdalene – but this is now in the Museo dell'Opera del Duomo (see entry).

Biblioteca Mediceo-Laurenziana

See San Lorenzo

Biblioteca Nazionale Centrale (National Library) K6

The large building of the National Library (built 1911–35) on Corso dei Tintori, Via Magliabechi and Piazza dei Cavalleggeri, near the Santa Croce complex (see entry), contains 24,721 manuscripts, 723,138 letters and documents, 3780 incunabula, over four million books, 5855 volumes and 4451 sheets of music, 630 atlases and 14,754 geographical and topographical maps.

Of especial value are an early 14th c. copy of Dante's "Divine Comedy" (probably the oldest in existence), manuscripts by Galileo, and missals and bibles dating from before the invention of printing. The library dates back to the 13th c. and preserves manuscripts by all the famous Florentines.

Location
Piazza dei Cavalleggeri

Buses
14, 19r, 23, 31, 32

Opening times
Mon.–Fri. 9 a.m.–7 p.m.,
Sat. 9 a.m.–1 p.m.

Boboli Gardens

See Giardino di Boboli

Brancacci Chapel

See Santa Maria del Carmine

Campanile

See Duomo Santa Maria del Fiore

Cappelle Medicee

See San Lorenzo

Casa di Bianca Capello　　　　　　　　　　　　　　　　H6
(House of Bianca Cappello; formerly the house of the Corbinelli)

Location
Via Maggio 26

Bianca Cappello was the daughter of a noble Venetian family and the sweetheart and later wife of Grand Duke Francesco I. Her house, which was completely rebuilt by Bernardo Buontalenti in 1567, is a fine example of the mansions lived in by the nobility of that time. It has an unusual feature in the grotesque representations of bats below the windows.

Casa Buonarroti (Michelangelo House and Museum)　　　K/L6

Location
Via Ghibellina 70

Bus
14

Opening times
Mon., Wed.–Sat.
9 a.m.–2 p.m.
Sun. and public holidays
9 a.m.–1 p.m.

Closed
Tues.

Michelangelo bought the house for his nephew Leonardo di Buonarroti but never lived in it himself. Leonardo's son, Michelangelo, decorated it and turned it into a memorial to the great artist. It was completely restored in 1964.

Two original sculptures by Michelangelo merit special attention: "Battle of the Centaurs and Lapiths", a marble relief which, although Michelangelo was only 17 when he created it, presages in the sense of movement and substantial nature of the figures, much of his later mastery; and "Madonna of the Steps" ("Madonna della Scala"), Michelangelo's earliest work, completed at the age of 16. The signs of genius are already clearly marked in the sense of space, the flow and counterflow on the steps on the left (hence the name, "Madonna of the Steps"), the fineness of the profile, the fall of the mantle.

The wooden crucifix (1494) from Santo Spirito (see entry), supposedly Michelangelo's earliest work for a church, is also interesting. Christ is depicted not as a man of sorrows but as a gentle handsome youth.

Other items on display are models or copies of the works of Michelangelo or mementoes of the artist's life. There are also sculptures and paintings by other masters.

Casa e Museo di Dante (Dante's House and Museum)　　　J/K6

Location
Via Dante Alighieri 4

Buses
14, 19, 23, 31, 32, 33

The houses that belonged to the Alighieri family are in Via Dante Alighieri. According to Florentine tradition one of them was the birthplace in 1265 of one of Florence's greatest sons, the poet Dante Alighieri who did not exactly find favour with his native city. Dante opposed the attempts by Pope Boniface

Casa Buonarroti

Casa di Dante

VII to incorporate Florence and the whole of Tuscany into the Papal States. When Charles de Valois was summoned to Florence by the Pope to treat for peace, Dante, as leader of the Ghibellines, was exiled from the city.

The museum contains photographs, editions of the "Divine Comedy", reproductions of Botticelli's drawing for Dante's work and portraits of the greatest of the Italian poets.

Cascine — A3–F5

W of the town the Cascine park extends more than 2 miles (3 km) along the Arno. Formerly farms belonging to the Medici and subsequently the Lorena family, the park was opened to the public by the Grand Dukes of Lorraine in the second half of the 18th c.

Its large race-course is one of the park's main attractions.

Buses
2, 9, 13r, 17, 26, 27

Casino di San Marco (Also Casino Mediceo) — K4

The palace on the site of the former Medici gardens was built by Bernardo Buontalenti in 1574 for Grand Duke Francesco I de' Medici who had his artist's studio and alchemist's laboratory here.

Today the building houses the Court of Appeal.

Location
Via Cavour 57

Buses
1, 6, 7, 10, 11, 17, 25

33

Cenacolo di Foligno (Foligno Refectory)   J5

Location
Via Faenza 42

Buses
1, 19n, 28, 34

Opening times
Sun. 9 a.m.–noon

The refectory of the former convent of St Onuphrius, which belonged to the Franciscan nuns of Foligno, contains Perugino's "Last Supper". It was seriously damaged in the 1966 flood. With this work Perugino proved that he was the equal in Florence of Andrea del Castagno and Ghirlandaio.

Cenacolo di San Salvi (St Salvi Refectory)   O6

Location
Via di S. Salvi 16

Buses
3, 6, 14, 34

Opening times
Sun. 9–noon

Andrea del Sarto's masterpiece, his version of the "Last Supper" in the Cenacolo di San Salvi, is well worth seeing. It is one of the finest early 16th c. frescoes in Florence.
The gallery in front of the refectory and the refectory itself also contain other works by Florentine masters. The monastery kitchen with its huge fireplace is also worth a visit.

*Cenacolo di Sant'Apollonia (Refectory of Sant'Apollonia)   J/K4/5

Location
Via XXVII Aprile 1

Buses
B, 1, 4, 6, 7, 10, 11, 17, 20, 25, 34

The former convent of Sant'Apollonia, which was secularised in 1808, then used as a military storehouse and which now houses part of the university, is worth visiting on account of its interesting church and the beautiful cloister with its graceful 15th c. columns.
The Coenaculum of St Apollonia, the convent's refectory, is now a museum.
The refectory of the Benedictine convent of Saint Apollonia, previously inaccessible because of the nun's seclusion, contains Andrea del Castagno's "Last Supper" (*c.* 1457). This fresco has an important place in Renaissance painting: the accuracy of its perspective and the realistic physical vigour of the figures (especially Jesus and the figure of Judas sitting apart from the others) make the picture intensely dramatic.
Also interesting are (above it) Castagno's "Crucifixion", "Entombment" and "Resurrection" and his two lunettes "Pietà" and "Christ crucified with the Virgin, St John and Saints".

*Certosa del Galluzzo (Carthusian Monastery)

Location
Galluzzo, 3 miles (5 km) S

Bus
41

The Carthusian monastery of Galluzzo is equally famed for its architecture and its works of art.
Niccolò Acciaiuoli, an important Florentine statesman and a friend of Petrarch and Boccaccio, had the monastery built in 1341 for the Carthusians, an anchorite order founded by St Bruno of Cologne. It contained blocks of individual cells for the

The Carthusian monastery of Certosa del Galluzzo

monks and common areas for prayers and services. In earlier days the monastery was richly endowed with art treasures, but Napoleon robbed the order of about 500 works of art and only a few were ever returned.

In two rooms of the art gallery there are examples of the once immense collection of art treasures on display, including four lunette frescoes of Christ's Passion by Pontormo (based on drawings by Dürer) and a "Madonna and Child" by Lucas Cranach.

The monastery buildings which, unlike those of other Orders, were not where the monks lived – their cells were in separate blocks – but where they assembled for communal activities include a parlatory, a medium-sized cloister, the chapter house, the "Great Cloister", the refectory, the "Small Cloister" and finally the pharmacy where the monastery's souvenirs and liqueurs are on sale.

In the late 18th and the early 19th c. Pope Pius VI and Pope Pius VII spent long periods in the Foresteria, the monastery's guest-house.

The church of San Lorenzo, which is worth seeing, is reached by crossing a large square. The Cappella di San Tobia (left of the high altar) contains the tomb of Niccolò Acciaiuoli and the tombstones of three other members of the Acciaiuoli family (including that of Lorenzo di Niccolò).

San Lorenzo (church)

In the Cappella di Sant'Andrea is the famous tomb of Cardinal Agnolo II Acciaiuoli, formerly ascribed to Donatello but now thought to be by Francesco da Sangallo.

35

Chiostro dello Scalzo (Cloister of the Discalced)   K4

Location
Via Cavour 69

Buses
1, 6, 7, 10, 11, 17, 25

Opening times
Sun, and public holidays
9 a.m.–noon (ring the bell)

The Chiostro dello Scalzo, a graceful cloister with slender columns, was decorated by Andrea del Sarto between 1514 and 1526 for the "Confraternity of St John the Baptist", whose crossbearers used to walk barefoot (scalzo) in processions. The famous frescoes depicting scenes from the life of John the Baptist have been restored several times.
The most important frescoes, all monochrome, are the Birth of John the Baptist (1526), the Sermon of St John (1515) and the Dance of Salome (1522).

Colonna della Croce al Trebbio (Column)   J5

Location
Via del Moro

Buses
6, 11, 36, 37

This granite column, which stands at the junction of Via del Moro, Via delle Belle Donne and Via del Trebbio, was erected in 1338. It has a fine Gothic capital, decorated with the symbols of the Evangelists, and a cross of the Pisan school.

Conservatorio Musicale Luigi Cherubini   K5
(Collection of old musical instruments)

Location
Via degli Alfani 80

Buses
B, 1, 4, 6, 7, 10, 11, 17, 25

The Conservatorio, founded in the early 19th c., houses a comprehensive music library and a collection of old musical instruments, including early pianos by the inventor of the pianoforte, Bartolomeo Cristofori, violins by the famous Italian violin-makers Stradivarius and Amati, and musical instruments from ancient Egypt and the Orient.
The collection was founded in the early 18th c. by Ferdinando, the son of Cosimo III. Cristofori was its curator and was also responsible for the most important acquisitions.

Dante Museum

See Casa e Museo di Dante

**Duomo Santa Maria del Fiore e Campanile   J/K5
(Cathedral of Santa Maria del Fiore and Campanile)

Location
Piazza del Duomo

Buses
1, 6, 7, 10, 11, 13r, 14, 17, 19r, 23, 25, 31, 32, 33

The cathedral of Florence is more than the symbol of the city. Together with the Campanile and the Baptistery (see Battistero) it forms one of the most magnificent works of art in the world. Florentines could not survive without a glimpse of the dome of their cathedral. It would seem that when Michelangelo was creating the dome of St Peter's he was seeking to transplant Brunelleschi's masterpiece from his native city of Florence to Rome.
At the end of the 13th c. the citizens of Florence, conscious of the growing importance of their city, wanted to erect a great new edifice on the site of the church of Santa Reparata that would surpass the other churches in the city in its beauty and

The dome of the cathedral – symbol of Florence

its dimensions. Famous architects, first Arnolfo di Cambio (from 1294), then Giotto, Andrea Pisano, Francesco Talenti and Giovanni Ghini made such progress with the building work despite numerous interruptions that between 1420 and 1434 Filippo Brunelleschi was able to crown it with the dome – that sensational feat of architectural bravura. In 1436 the cathedral was dedicated to St Mary the Virgin and acquired the epithet "del Fiore" from the lily on Florence's coat of arms.

The present ornate façade, designed by Emilio de Fabris', was not added until 1875–87. (The old façade, which had never been completed, was demolished in 1587.) The cathedral has some impressive dimensions. It is 526·28 ft (160·45 m) long; the nave is 141 ft (43 m) wide; the transept 298 ft (91 m) wide; the façade is 164 ft (50 m) high; the dome is 375·1 ft (114·36 m) high and 149·31 ft (45·52 m) in diameter. The church's 89,308 sq. ft (8300 sq. m) of floor space can take about 25,000 people. Santa Maria del Fiore is Italy's third largest church after St Peter's in Rome and Milan Cathedral.

Exterior

The main feature of the exterior is the rich articulation with coloured marble – white from Carrara, green from Prato and red from the Maremma. There is marble everywhere – on the façade built in the medieval Gothic style, on the sides of the aisles leading to the nave, on the buttresses, the small side domes and the massive main dome.

Dome
In his building of the dome Brunelleschi gambled on creating a structural masterpiece (with modest wisdom he commended

it to the protection of the Virgin) which is both powerful and aesthetically pleasing. The white ribs that meet at the lantern clearly outline the contours of the red covering of the dome.

The streets behind the apse offer an impressive view of the mountain of marble that is the cathedral and Brunelleschi's dome. At this point there is a gallery on the drum of the dome. This was built at the time of Michelangelo who was intensely critical of it, voicing the opinion that it looked like a "cricket cage".

In the pavement in front of the apse is a marble slab marking the spot where on 17 January 1600 the gilded ball from the dome hit the ground and shattered after it had been struck by lightning. It was replaced by a larger one below the cross.

The lantern, too, was often a victim of lightning but was unremittingly repaired. Today it is protected by a modern lightning conductor. (Visitors may climb up inside the dome as far as the lantern; the stairs start from the left aisle.)

Sculpture

The exterior has an abundance of sculpted figures: on the top spandrel of the façade "God the Father", with, immediately below, busts of famous Florentine artists; under a huge rose window "Virgin and Child" and statues of the apostles; below that in the niches of the four pillars are bishops of Florence and Pope Eugene IV who consecrated the church in 1436. The bronze doors have reliefs of Mary and allegorical figures of the Christian virtues.

Portals

While walking round the cathedral it is well worth having a look at the four portals.

On the right-hand side near the Campanile:

Porta del Campanile, with "Christ giving a Blessing" in the gable and "Madonna and Child" in the lunette, both in the style of Andrea Pisano.

Porta dei Canonici. Above the "Porch of the Canons" is a "Virgin and Child" by Lorenzo di Giovanni d'Ambrogio.

Nearby are the memorials to the architects Arnolfo di Cambio and Brunelleschi and a stone with the inscription "Sasso di Dante" marking the spot where the poet is supposed to have watched the cathedral being built.

On the left side:

'Porta della Balla" (late 14th c.). The door has a polychrome "Madonna and Child and two Angels". The twisted columns at the sides are supported by lions.

"Porta della Mandorla." The finest portal in the church, this "Porch of the Glory" was designed by Giovanni d'Ambrogio and Nanni and completed by various artists (Donatello, Niccolò di Pietro Lamberti and Ghirlandaio). Above the door in the "almond" is the Virgin borne up by angels (1421, by Nanni di Banco); in the lunette is a mosaic of the "Annunciation" by Domenico and Davide Ghirlandaio (1491).

Interior of the church

Severity and beauty are also the theme of the interior of the cathedral which makes its impact through its Gothic forms, its soaring arches and pillars, untrammelled by gaudy ornamenta-

Elaborate decoration on the façade of the cathedral of Santa Maria del Fiore ▶

Duomo Santa Maria del Fiore e Campanile

E side of the cathedral

Fresco above the main door

tion to detract from the feeling of spaciousness (later additions were removed during restoration), while the sense of severity is heightened by the earthy hue of the stonework.

The ground plan of the cathedral is a Latin cross with a nave and two aisles; the space beneath the dome is enlarged by its extension into the three surrounding apses.

Despite its bare aspect, the interior has some rich and precious figures.

Front

The three stained-glass windows above the main portals depicting St Stephen (left), the Assumption of the Virgin (centre) and St Laurence (right) were designed by Lorenzo Ghiberti and executed by Niccolò di Piero.

Above the central door is a mosaic depicting the Coronation of the Virgin (*c.* 1300, by Gaddo Gaddi) together with the famous clock with hands that move anticlockwise. The heads of prophets in the corners were painted in by Paolo Uccello in 1443.

Right of the main portal is the Gothic tomb of Bishop Antonio d'Orso (d. 1321) by Tino da Camaino (incomplete; various parts in the Museo Nazionale del Bargello, see Palazzo del Bargello).

North aisle

In the first marble recess is a statue of Joshua (early 15th c.) by Bernardo Ciuffagni, Donatello and Nanni di Bartoli.

Opposite the second pillar is a fresco transferred on to canvas by Niccolò da Tolentino (1456).

Duomo Santa Maria del Fiore

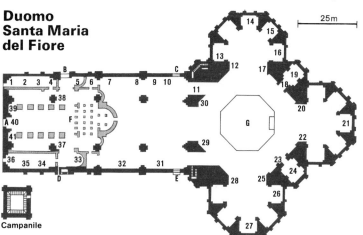

Campanile

A Portale Maggiore with relief "Maria in Gloria", by A. Passaglia

B Porta della Balla

C Porta della Mandorla, by Giovanni d'Ambrogio and Nanni. Above the portal, Nanni di Banco's Virgin borne up by angels

D Porta del Campanile with Annunciation

E Porta dei Canonici, above "Madonna col Bambino", by d'Ambrogio

F Cripta di Santa Reparata, remains of old cathedral

G Brunelleschi's dome with fresco of the Last Judgement by Vasari and precious stained-glass windows

1 Window "S. Stefano e due Angeli", by Ghiberti

2 Bust of Emilio de Fabis, designer of the façade, by V. Consani (1887)

3 Statue of Joshua (head by Donatello)

4 Bust of Arnolfo di Cambio, by U. Cambi (1843)

5 Bust of the organist Squarcialupi, by Benedetto da Maiano (1490)

6 Equestrian figure of Niccolò da Tolentino, painted by A. del Castagno (1456)

7 Equestrian figure of Giovanni Acuto (John Hawkwood), painted by P. Uccello (1436)

8 Window dated 1395. Below in the marble recess a statue of

King David (B. Ciuffagni, 1434)

9 "Santi Cosma e Damiano", by Bicci di Lorenzo (15th c.)

10 14th c. window, below, "Dante and the Divine Comedy", by D. di Michelino (1456)

11 Stairs up to the dome

12 "S. Tommaso", by De' Rossi, 16th c. statue

13 "S. Giuseppe", painting by Lorenzo di Credi

14 Marble altar (Buggiano)

15 "Madonna with Saints", altarcloth in the style of P. Bonaguida

16 "Pietà", by Michelangelo (1550/1553)

17 "S. Andrea", by A. Ferrucci, statue (16th c.)

18 In the door lunette, "Risurrezione", terracotta, by Luca della Robbia (1444). Bronze door, also by della Robbia, assisted by Michelozzo and Maso di Bartolomeo

19 Sagrestia nuova o delle Messe

20 "S. Pietro", by B. Bandinelli, statue (16th c.)

21 Above the altar, two angels carrying candles (Luca della Robbia, 1450). Below the altar, reliquary of St Zenobius (Ghiberti, 1432–42)

22 "S. Giovanni", by B. da Rovezzano, statue (16th c.)

23 In the lunette, "Resurrection"

in enamelled terracotta, by Luca della Robbia (1450)

24 Sagrestia vecchia o dei canonici

25 "S. Giacomo Minore", by G. Bandini, 16th c. statue

26 Fragment of a fresco in the style of Giotto, "Madonna del Popolo"

27 Michelozzo's altar

28 "S. Filippo", by G. Bandini, 16th c. statue

29 "S. Matteo", by De' Rossi, 16th c. statue

30 "S. Giacomo Maggiore", by J. Sansovino, 16th c. statue

31 Bust of the philosopher Marsilio Ficino, by A. Ferrucci (1521)

32 In the marble recess, a statue of Isaiah, by B. Ciuffagni (1427)

33 "S. Bartolomeo in Trono", by R. di Jacopo Franchi

34 Roundel, by B. da Maiano, showing Giotto at work

35 Bust of Brunelleschi, by A. Cavalcanti

36 Window "S. Lorenzo e Angeli", by Ghiberti

37 Stairs down to the Cripta di Santa Reparata

38 Recess, with St Zanobius stamping out pride and cruelty, by G. del Biondo (late 14th c.)

39 Tomb of Antonio d'Orso

40 "L'Assunta", window, designed by Ghiberti

41 "Incoronazione di Maria", mosaic, by G. Gaddi

41

To the right of this is the equestrian figure of John Hawkwood (Giovanni Acuto in Italian), commander of the Florentine mercenary army, painted by Paolo Uccello (1436) to imitate sculpture.

In the next marble recess is the statue of King David made for the façade by Bernardo Ciuffagni (1434).

Below the window is a painting by Domenico di Michelino glorifying Dante (1465), a late rehabilitation of the poet by the city that once sent him into exile.

The staircase that leads up to the dome starts from the point where the aisle joins the apse. There is a marvellous panoramic view from the lantern.

North apse (or "Tribune")

The N apse is divided into five chapels. The stained-glass windows were designed by Ghiberti.

In the fourth chapel is an interesting double-sided retable in the style of Pacino di Buonaguida depicting the "Madonna and Saints" and "Annunciation and Saints".

In the pavement is Toscanelli's gnomon which since 1468 has been used for astronomical calculations such as the summer solstice, indicted by the sun's rays which, on 21 June, shine down through a conical hole in the lantern of the dome precisely on to this metal plate.

Dome

On the inner surface of the dome (undergoing restoration) is the great fresco of the Last Judgement by Giorgio Vasari (begun in 1572 and completed by Frederico Zuccari in 1578). The stained glass in the round windows of the drum was executed from cartoons by Ghiberti, Paolo Uccello and Andrea del Castagno.

At the foot of the pillars supporting the drum are eight statues of apostles. Against the first pillar on the left stand St James the Greater by Jacopo Sansovino and St Thomas by Vincenzo de Rossi, and against the second pillar on the left stand St Andrew by Andrea Ferrucci and St Peter by Baccio Bandinelli. On the opposite side the third pillar on the right has St John by Benedetto da Rovezzano and St James the Less by Giovanni Bandini and against the fourth pillar on the right are St Philip, also by Giovanni Bandini, and Vincenzo de Rossi's St Matthew.

Choir

Under the dome is the choir with the high altar. The octagonal marble balustrade is based on a design by Baccio d'Agnolo; the 88 reliefs decorating it are by Baccio and Giovanni Bandinelli. The high altar (by Baccio Bandinelli) and the crucifix (by Benedetto da Maiano; 1495–7) are also of interest.

New Sacristy

The sacristies are especially interesting. In the lunette above the door of the new Sacristy is a glazed terracotta "Resurrection of Christ" by Luca della Robbia (1444).

The fine bronze door is also the work of Luca della Robbia (with Michelozzo). Its ten panels depict Mary with the Infant Jesus, John the Baptist, Evangelists and early Fathers.

This sacristy is where Lorenzo the Magnificent took refuge in 1478 when he and his brother were attacked during a service in the cathedral on the day of the Pazzi conspiracy. Lorenzo managed to escape but his brother Giuliano perished.

Central apse
In the Cappella di San Zenobio (Chapel of St Zenobius) in the central apse is a fine bronze urn by Lorenzo Ghiberti containing the relics of the saint.

Old Sacristy
Above the door of the Old Sacristy ("dei Canonici", "of the Canons") is a terracotta relief of the "Ascension of Christ" by Luca della Robbia. In the sacristy can be found a piscina by Buggiano, Lorenzo di Credi's "Archangel Michael" and two terracotta candlesticks in the form of angels, also by Luca della Robbia.

South apse (or "Tribune")
The S apse is also divided into five chapels.
The first chapel (after the Old Sacristy) contains an interesting fresco by Giotto: "Madonna del Popolo".
The details of the statues against the pillars supporting the drum are given in the section on the dome.

South aisle
Interesting features here include a bust below the window of Marsilio Ficino (1521), the great Renaissance philosopher, and a medallion depicting Giotto by Benedetto da Maiano (1490; opposite the last pillar).
Next to it in a wooden recess is the statue of the prophet Isaiah by Nanni di Banco (1408) and a medallion of Brunelleschi. This is the work of Andrea Cavalcanti, known as Buggiano, who was the heir and favourite pupil of Brunelleschi.
The door leading out to the Campanile is also in this aisle.

* * Campanile (bell-tower)

One of the great landmarks of Florence, the Campanile, the cathedral belfry, 269 ft (82 m) high and 47·6 ft (14·5 m) wide, was begun in 1334 by Giotto (di Bordone). After his death in 1337, Andrea Pisano continued the building of the belfry in accordance with Giotto's plans but his successor, Francesco Talenti, deviated from the original design. The tower was completed in 1387. It is well worth while climbing the 414 steps for the splendid view of the city from the top.
The building is characterised by the harmony of its dimensions, the strength of the octagonal pillars, the delicate articulation of the intervening walls and the intricate alternation of the colours of the marble.
On the lowest storey are two rows of panels containing allegorical bas-reliefs. Most of the hexagonal panels are by Andrea Pisano, who worked to Giotto's designs, and Luca della Robbia. They depict the life of Man, his work and his art.
The lozenge-shaped panels in the second row contain allegories of planets, virtues, liberal arts and sacraments.
The niches in the second storey above these lozenges used to contain statues of saints, prophets and sibyls sculpted between 1300 and 1400 by Florentine artists (including Donatello). Today these are kept in the Museo dell'Opera del Duomo (see entry) to protect them against pollution. There are copies in some of the niches.

Opening times
Mon., Wed., Fri. 9.30 a.m.–1 p.m., 2–5 p.m.; Sun. and public holidays 10 a.m.–1 p.m.

*Fiesole

The little town, 968 ft (295 m) above the Arno, was settled by Etruscans as early as the 7th and 6th c. B.C., and later by the Romans (Faesulae). Fiesole declined in importance after it suffered defeat at the hands of Florence.

It is worth making a trip to Fiesole not only for the splendid view of Florence from the hilltops of San Francesco and Sant'Apollinare but also because of the sights that the town itself has to offer.

Fiesole's main square, the broad Piazza Mino da Fiesole, is on the site of the old Roman forum. Around the square there are several fine buildings, particularly the cathedral with its soaring bell-tower, the Museo Bandini, the Palazzo Vescovile (Bishop's Palace) dating back to the 11th c. with a 17th c. façade, and the Seminary, the church of Santa Maria Primerana and the Palazzo Pretorio (today the town hall).

Location
5 miles (8 km) NE

Bus
7

Museo Civico (archaeological museum)

Fiesole's museum contains numerous finds from the Etruscan and Roman period which have come from local excavations or have been presented to the museum; the exhibits include a stele (470–460 B.C.; with funeral meal, dancing and animal fights), the head of Emperor Claudius (A.D. 41–54) and a statue of Dionysius (Roman copy of a Greek original).

Location
Via Giovanni Dupré

Opening times
Tues.–Sat. 10 a.m.–12.30 p.m., 2–5 p.m.

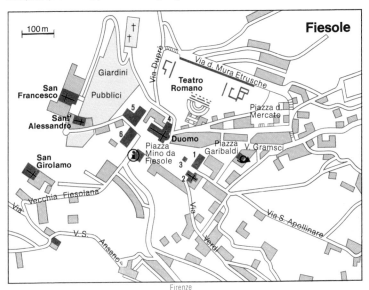

1 Palazzo Pretorio	3 „L'Incontro di Teano"
2 Santa Maria Primerana	4 Museo Bandini

5 Palazzo Vescovile
6 Seminario

◄ Giotto's Campanile: the bell-tower of the cathedral

Fiesole

Badia Fiesolana (abbey)

The Badia was the cathedral church of Fiesole until the 11th c.
when it was handed over to Benedictine monks and became
known as an "abbey". The church and monastery were
completely reconstructed during the Renaissance. The interior
(in the style of Brunelleschi) is impressively severe.
The Romanesque façade of the original church was inspired by
the unfinished 15th c. façade.
Fra Angelico lived in the Dominican monastery near the Badia
before he made his name as a painter in Florence.

Museo Bandini

Location
Piazza Mino

Opening times
Tues.–Sat. 9.30 a.m.–
12.30 p.m., 2–5 p.m.

In 1795 Canon Angiolo Maria Bandini, librarian of the
Biblioteca Mediceo-Laurenziana (see entry) and an eminent
scientist, started collecting works of art which after his death
were placed at the disposal of the cathedral chapter of Fiesole.
His collection of religious art, including many pictures of saints,
has found a worthy resting place in the small museum.

Duomo (cathedral)

The church of San Romolo became the episcopal church when
the Badia was handed over to the Benedictine monks. The
cathedral has succeeded in preserving its original medieval
atmosphere. It was begun in 1028 and extended in the 13th c.
(around the 138·7 ft (42·3 m) high machicolated campanile).
Inside are several interesting works of art, particularly the
frescoes and sculptures in the Cappella Salutati.

Teatro Romano e Terme (Roman theatre and baths)

Opening times
Tues.–Sat. 9.30 a.m.–
12.30 p.m., 2–5 p.m.

Closed
Mon.

Behind the cathedral a small street leads to the Roman theatre,
built in the early days of the Roman Empire and enlarged during
the reigns of Emperors Claudius and Septimius Severus. The
semicircular theatre, which is 112 ft (34 m) in diameter seats
3000 people. Plays were performed on a stage 86·6 ft (26·4 m)
long, 4·43 ft (1·35 m) high and 21 ft (6·4 m) deep.
Behind the Roman theatre are the ruins of the baths, built under
Sulla and enlarged during the reign of Hadrian. Although the
arches supported by huge pillars have always been visible, the
whole of the complex was not excavated until 1891–2.

Sant'Alessandro (church)

Next to the park is the church of Sant'Alessandro. The saint to
whom it is dedicated was a bishop of Fiesole. The church is
built over an old Etruscan temple that was later replaced by a
Roman temple to Bacchus. Early in the 6th c. Emperor
Theodoric converted the building into a Christian church
which was remodelled in the early 19th c.

Fiesole: The Roman theatre

San Francesco (church)

Above the park in a picturesque square on top of a hill (1131 ft – 345 m) is the 14th c. church of San Francesco which in 1407 was handed over to the Franciscans.

Villa Medici

Outside Fiesole is the Villa Medici, also known as Belcanto or Il Palagio di Fiesole, built 1458–61, probably by the architect Michelozzo for Cosimo the Elder.
This is where the Pazzi conspirators had originally planned to murder Lorenzo de' Medici and his brother Giuliano (1478) before deciding that a more suitable place would be the Duomo Santa Maria del Fiore (see entry).

Forte (Fortezza) del Belvedere (Also Forte di San Giorgio)   J7

The massive fort above Florence on the left bank of the Arno was the work of the architect Buontalenti (1590–5), probably based on plans drawn up by Giovanni de' Medici. It was commissioned by Grand Duke Ferdinando I who intended it to serve as a stronghold where he could safeguard his family and all their riches. Inside is a small palace, also designed by Buontalenti, which today is used for temporary exhibitions.
The ramparts of the star-shaped bastion near the Porta San Giorgio (see entry) afford a splendid view of the city.

Location
Costa di San Giorgio/Van San Leonardo

Buses
13, 38

Fortezza da Basso (Or di San Giovanni Battista)   H/J4

Location
Viale Filippo Strozzi

Buses
1, 4, 7, 10, 14, 17, 19r, 22,
23, 25, 28, 31, 32, 33

The vast five-sided fortress near the main station, today used as a barracks, was designed in 1534 by Antonio Sangallo the Younger and built under the direction of Pier Francesco da Viterbo and Alessandro Vitelli (1534–5). With this bastion Alessandro de' Medici sought to manifest and consolidate his power after his return to the city.

Fountain of Neptune

See Piazza della Signoria

Galleria dell'Accademia (Academy Art Gallery)   K5

Location
Via Ricasoli 52

Buses
B, 1, 4, 6, 7, 10, 11, 17, 25

Opening times
Tues.–Sat. 9 a.m.–2 p.m.,
Sun. and public holidays
9 a.m.–1 p.m.

Closed
Mon.

The spacious rooms of the hospital of St Matthew near the former church of San Matteo house the "Academy", the Galleria dell'Accademia, founded in 1784 by Grand Duke Pietro Leopoldo I of Lorraine. Together with the other famous art galleries of Florence (in the Palazzo degli Uffizi and Palazzo Pitti – see entries), it houses tapestries and important paintings of the Florentine school from the 13th to 16th c.

Many pictures are not yet in their final positions, but it should be possible to see the following:
Room 2: Early Renaissance works of the Florentine school.
Room 3: "Madonna" by Botticelli.
Room 5: Duccio's "Christ crucified" and "Tree of the Cross".
Room 6: "Madonna and Child with two Angels and four Saints" by Orcagna. "Trinity" by Nardo di Cione.
Room 7: "Coronation of the Virgin" by Jacopo di Cione, "Pietà" by Giovanni da Milano, scenes from the lives of Christ and St Francis by Taddeo Gaddi.

Works by Michelangelo
The Academy's main claim to fame is for its sculptures by Michelangelo, with his "David" taking pride of place. It was removed from its original location in the Piazza della Signoria (see entry) in 1873 and set up here to protect it from the ravages of the weather (traces of this are still visible). The statue in the Piazza is a copy.
At the age of 26 Michelangelo had accepted a huge block of marble which had been rejected by others because of its proportions – it was over 13 ft (4 m) high but not very "deep". He worked on it from 1501 to 1504 to produce a figure of youthful energy and beauty, his "David", who, according to the Bible, was an Israelite shepherd-boy who emerged victorious from his seemingly hopeless battle with the giant Goliath.
Even Michelangelo's contemporaries praised his statue's virtues: the perfect harmony of the body, the noble posture of the head, the alert and confident expression on the face, the tension of the warrior and the tranquillity of the future victor. The David became the symbol of the spirit of liberty in Florence, the irrepressible urge for independence of its citizens and their political body, the Signoria. During the disturbances in the city

Galleria dell'Accademia: Michelangelo's "Slaves" and "David" (in the background)

in 1527 (when the Medici were driven out) David's left arm was smashed but the fragments were gathered up and reassembled.

To the right of the David is a bronze portrait of Michelangelo by Daniele da Volterra, probably the most authentic of the known portraits of the artist.

The Accademia is the place where, in the uncompleted figures of the Slaves, St Matthew and Pietà di Palestrina, it is possible to follow most closely Michelangelo's creative process as a sculptor.

Michelangelo intended the "Slaves" for the tomb of Pope Julius II in Rome. He spent from 1519 to 1536 working on six statues but was unable to complete them. After his death they were set up in the Giardino di Boboli (see entry). Four of them are now in the Academy – the "Awakener", the "Bearded One", the "Young One" and the "Atlas" (the other two are in the Louvre in Paris).

Before 1505 Michelangelo sculpted St Matthew, one of the apostles planned for the tomb of Julius II. It was the only one of the twelve he even started and though not completed it is highly expressive. The finished parts of the statue blend into the unhewn sections of the marble to form a whole.

Galleria d'Arte Moderna (Gallery of Modern Art)

See Palazzo Pitti

Galleria Corsini

See Palazzo Corsini

Galleria Palatina or Pitti

See Palazzo Pitti

Galleria degli Uffizi (Collection of paintings)

See Palazzo degli Uffizi

*Giardino di Boboli (Boboli Gardens)   H/J7

Location
Piazza Pitti

Buses
11, 36, 37

Opening times
9 a.m.–5.30 p.m. daily; May–
August 9 a.m.–6.30 p.m.

Admission free

Behind the Palazzo Pitti (entrance) and between the Forte di
Belvedere and the Porta Romana (see entries) can be found the
111 acres (45 hectares) of the Boboli Gardens which owe their
name to the Bogoli or Bogolini family. Work on this splendid
park, perfect for long walks, was begun between 1550 and
1560 by Niccolò de' Pericoli (known as "Tribolo" – the
tormented), continued by Bernardo Buontalenti (1585–8) and
completed by Alfonso Parigi the Younger (1628–58).

There are various interesting features in the gardens, considered to be one of the finest Mannerist sites of its kind:

Cavaliere Garden: Monkey Fountain

Fontana del Bacco

Fontana del Bacco (Fountain of Bacchus)
The figure riding on a tortoise represents the court dwarf of
Cosimo I.

Grotta di Buontalenti
Created by Buontalenti (1533–88), the grotto has statues of
Ceres and Apollo, plaster casts of Michelangelo's "Slaves" and
a Venus by Giambologna.

Amphitheatre
Built in 1618 by Giulio and Alfonso Parigi and reconstructed in
1700, the amphitheatre was used by the Grand Dukes for their
magnificent festivities. The obelisk comes from Egypt and the
granite basin from Rome.

Neptune Fountain
Neptune (by Stoldo Lorenzi, 1565) stands on a rock
surrounded by Tritons and Sirens.

Statue of Abundance
The colossal figure of "Abundance" is by Giambologna and
Pietro Tacca.

Giardino del cavaliere ("Garden of the Cavalier")
The terrace on the old city wall ramparts is the site of Tacca's
Monkey Fountain.

Museo delle Porcellane (porcelain museum)

The museum contains Italian, French and German porcelain
and a collection from Vienna formerly in the possession of the
Grand Dukes of Tuscany.

Opening times
Tues.–Sat. 9 a.m.–2 p.m.,
Sun. 9 a.m.–1 p.m.

Viottolone
This is the name of an avenue leading from the Giardino del
Cavaliere to the Piazzale dell'Isolotto. It is lined with cypresses,
chestnut oaks and parasol pines.

Piazzale dell'Isolotto
In the centre of the oval square (laid out in 1618) is a pool with,
in the centre, a copy of Giambologna's Fountain of Oceanus
(original in the Museo Nazionale del Bargello, see Palazzo del
Bargello).

Loggia del Bigallo J5

This typical late-Gothic building near the Duomo and the
Battistero (see entries) was commissioned by the Confraternity
of Mercy (Compagnia della Misericordia) as a place to
"display" lost or abandoned children for adoption. The marble
loggia and the little palace of which it is part were built between
1353 and 1358 (probably by Ambrogio di Renzo). In 1445
Ventura di Moro and Rossello di Jacopo Franchi painted the
walls under the double arches with frescoes of scenes from the
life of St Peter, but the ones there now are only copies. Some
of the originals are to be seen in the town hall inside the palace,
which also houses works of 14th and 15th c. Florentine artists.

Location
Piazza S. Giovanni

Buses
6, 11

Opening times
2–7 p.m. daily

Loggia dei Lanzi   J6

Location
Piazza della Signoria

Buses
14, 19, 23, 31, 32

Opening times
Tues.–Sat. 9 a.m.–2 p.m.,
Sun. 9 a.m.–1 p.m.

Closed
Mon.

Also known as the Loggia della Signoria, the Loggia dei Lanzi owes its name to the guard of German lancers stationed here by Cosimo I.
Known, too, as the Loggia dell'Orcagna (after the famous artist Orcagna who may well have designed it), it was built between 1376 and 1382 under the direction of Benci di Cione and Simone di Francesco Talenti. The arcade, one of the finest examples of Florentine Gothic architecture, was used by the Republic for official ceremonies. This is where ambassadors and princes were received and where the Priors and the Gonfaloniere were formally proclaimed.
With the fall of the Republic the Loggia lost this political function and assumed a purely decorative role. After it was restored in the last century it resumed its original official use, and is now once again decked out with tapestries and garlands on festive occasions.

Exterior

Above the round arches are panels with allegorical figures of the cardinal and theological virtues made by various artists to designs by Agnolo Gaddi (1384–9). On the roof is a terrace from which there is access to the Uffizi Gallery (see Palazzo e Galleria degli Uffizi).

Museum

Inside the arcade is a small museum containing some important sculptures.
To the right and left of the entrance are two lions, one from Classical Greece and the other a 16th c. copy (Vacca).

Loggia dei Lanzi: the arcade

On a clockwise tour of the museum the visitor's gaze immediately falls on the bronze statue of Perseus by Benvenuto Cellini (1545–54), an impressive masterpiece because of its delicacy of workmanship and bold composition.

In the centre of the wall diagonally opposite is the "Rape of Polyxena" in marble by Pio Ferdi (1866), followed by Classical statues of women along the back wall (very much restored). In the centre of the other side is another marble group, Giambologna's "Hercules fighting with Nessus the Centaur" (1599).

At the front is another masterpiece, "The Rape of the Sabines", a lively marble group of figures also by Giambologna (1583). It is said that the work was not given this title until later, so the artist was clearly chiefly making use of the theme of youthful manly strength, womanly beauty and old age to demonstrate his skill and his art.

* Loggia di Mercato Nuovo (Loggia of the New Market)   J6

The Loggia di Mercato Nuovo, built by Del Tasso (1547–51) and formerly frequented by silk-merchants and goldsmiths, is today the market for Florentine handicrafts. The hall, which is open on all sides, is supported by 20 columns.

Next to it is the "Fontana del Porcellino" or "Fountain of the Little Pig" as Pietro Tacca's bronze wild boar (1612) is popularly known. Tourist throw coins into the fountain and make a wish to return to Florence.

Location
Via di Porta Rossa

Buses
B, 6, 11, 14, 19, 23, 31, 32

Loggia di San Paolo   H5

Opposite the church of Santa Maria Novella (see entry), on the S side of the square, is the Loggia di San Paolo which was commissioned in 1466 by the head of the Ospedale di San Paolo. It is modelled closely on Brunelleschi's Loggia degli Innocenti (the Porch of the Foundling Hospital). The columns were replaced in 1789. It is decorated with terracotta medallions by the Florentine artists Andrea and Giovanni della Robbia.

Location
Piazza Santa Maria Novella

Buses
9, 13, 14, 17, 19, 22, 23, 36, 37

Medici Chapel

See San Lorenzo, Cappelle Medicee

Michelangelo House and Museum

See Casa Buonarroti

Monumento di Carlo Goldoni (Carlo Goldoni Memorial)   H6

The monument to the famous Italian dramatist Carlo Goldoni (1707–93), erected here by Ulisse Cambi in 1873, is the main feature of the square by the Arno, where seven streets converge, which bears the Venetian comedy playwright's name.

Location
Piazza Goldoni

Mosaic Museum

See Opificio e Museo delle Pietre Dure

Museo dell'Antica Casa Fiorentina (Museum of the Old Florentine House)

See Palazzo Davanzati

*Museo Archeologico Centrale dell'Etruria   K5
(Archaeological Museum)

Location
Piazza SS. Annunziata 9b

Buses
1, 4, 6, 7, 10, 11, 17, 25, 34

Opening times
Tues.–Sat. 9 a.m.–2 p.m.,
Sun. and public holidays
9 a.m.–1 p.m.

Closed
Mon.

This is the most important archaeological museum in Northern Italy. Founded in 1870 its principal exhibits are finds from the areas of Italy settled by the Etruscans, as well as Egyptian, Greek and Roman antiquities. Collections begun by the Medici family are kept here. It is housed in the Palazzo della Crocetta which was built in 1620 for the Grand Duchess Maria Magdalena of Austria.

The museum is divided into the Egyptian Museum and the Museum of Etruscan, Greek and Roman Archaeology (Antiquarium etrusco-greco-romano).

SECONDO PIANO

PRIMO PIANO

Museo Archeologico

SECOND FLOOR (SECONDO PIANO)
    Museum of Etruscan, Greek and Roman Archaeology (continuation)
  1, 2 Prehistoric department
  3–6 Italian and Mediterranean comparisons
 7–15 Vases of various origins, Etruscan terracottas and sculptures
   16 Temporarily closed
17–30 Etruscan urns, sarcophagi, objects found in tombs, wall-paintings

FIRST FLOOR (PRIMO PIANO)
  1–8 Museo Egiziano (Egyptian Museum): statues, reliefs, papyri, amulets, sarcophagi, mummies, a chariot made of Syrian wood
 9–22 Museum of Etruscan, Greek and Roman Archaeology: Etruscan scuptures, sarcophagi, bronzes, coins, jewellery

The Egyptian Museum, which ranks second in importance to the one in Turin, has statues, busts, ceramics, reliefs, sarcophagi, mummies, pictures and utensils from various Egyptian dynasties, including a very well-preserved wooden chariot (from the time of Rameses I, 14th c. B.C.).

Egyptian Museum

The Etrusco-Graeco-Roman department has displays of Etruscan urns and sarcophagi, including the Ramta Uzenai marble sarcophagus from Tarquinia; Etruscan, Greek and Roman bronzes, including the famous "Idolino" – the Greek statue of a young ephebe, a young man undergoing military training, (5th c. B.C.), the "Horse's Head" – a Greek bronze from the Roman period, the "Chimaera" – an Etruscan bronze with the body of a lion, the head of a ram and a serpent's tail, the "Orator" (dedicated to Aulus Metellus, 3rd c. B.C.) and a statue of Minerva, a copy of a Greek work found in Arezzo in 1554.

Antiquarium etrusco-greco-romano

Also of interest: the coin rooms with collections of coins minted in Etruria, medieval and modern Roman coins, and Italian coins; the collection of precious stones with gems, cameos and gold and silver articles, and the collection of vases with the famous "François Vase", painted by Klitias in the studio of the Greek Ergotimos (6th c. B.C.).
Also worth seeing: the Etruscan Gallery of Plaster Casts, the Gallery of Etruscan Painting, the collection of hieroglyphics begun by Lorenzo de' Medici (the Magnificent) and the prehistoric department.

Other collections

Museo degli Argenti (Silver Collection)

See Palazzo Pitti

Museo Bardini (Bardini Museum)   K7

The Bardini Museum houses sculptures, paintings, furniture, ceramics, tapestries, arms, etc. from the Classical, Renaissance and Baroque periods. The collection was bequeathed to the city of Florence in 1923 by the art dealer Stefano Bardini. It is now on show to the public in the 19th c. palace where he lived. Among the interesting works are a Caritas, an allegory of Love by Tino di Camaino and three by Donatello; also a small plaster "Deposition" by Michelangelo.
The museum is closed on Wednesdays.

Location
Piazza de' Mozzi 1

Buses
13n, 19, 23r, 31, 32, 33

Opening times
Mon., Tues., Thurs.–Sat.
9 a.m.–2 p.m., Sun. and
public holidays 8 a.m.–1 p.m.

Museo delle Carrozze (Coach Museum)

See Palazzo Pitti

Museo della Fondazione Horne (Horne Museum)   K6

The English art critic Herbert Percy Horne (1864–1916) gave the State a valuable collection of paintings, sculptures, drawings, furniture and ancient ornaments and utensils which

Location
Via de' Benci 6

Museo Mediceo

Buses
13r, 14, 19, 23, 31, 32

Opening times
Mon.–Fri. 9 a.m.–1 p.m.

Closed
Sat.

are now on display in the Palazzetto Horne.
This building, also transferred to the State, was built in the late 15th c. for the Alberti family, probably by Simone del Pollaiolo ("Cronaca"), and later belonged to the Corsi family. The collection was seriously damaged in the 1966 floods (especially the exhibits on the ground floor. The rooms are currently being restored). The first floor houses 14th–16th c. paintings, including works by Simone Martini, Benozzo Gozzoli, Pietro Lorenzetti, Filippino Lippi and Bernardo Daddi.
Among the exhibits on the second floor are furniture made in Florence, drawings, roundels and terracottas (all 15th/16th c.).

Museo Mediceo (Medici Museum)

See Palazzo Medici-Riccardi

Museo Nazionale di Antropologia ed Etnologia (Museum of Mankind)

See Palazzo Nonfinito

Museo Nazionale del Bargello (National Museum)

See Palazzo del Bargello e Museo National

**Museo dell'Opera del Duomo (Cathedral Museum)   K5

Location
Piazza del Duomo 9

Buses
1, 6, 7, 10, 11, 13r, 14, 17, 19r, 22, 23, 25, 32, 33

Opening times
Mon.–Sat. 9.30 a.m.–1 p.m., 2–5 p.m.; Sun. and public holidays 10 a.m.–1 p.m.

A host of artists created notable works of art – sculpture, articles in gold and silver, embroidery, etc. – to furnish the Cathedral, the Campanile and the Baptistery (see entries). These could not be allowed to remain in their original positions because they were at risk from the weather and on security grounds so at an early stage they were removed for safekeeping. Since 1891 they have been kept in the Cathedral Museum, which since the 15th c. had also served as studios and workshops for the artists and craftsmen working on the cathedral.
Some of the most interesting exhibits are mentioned below.

Ground floor

Entrance
Above the portal of the Museo dell'Opera del Duomo (named after the cathedral building works) is a bust of Grand Duke Cosimo I (1572, by Giovanni Bandini).

Anteroom
Among the items in the anteroom is a bust of Brunelleschi, the creator of the dome of the cathedral.

"Room of the old façade of the cathedral"
This room contains statues that were incorporated in the old façade of the cathedral and which were removed before it was demolished in 1587. There is also a drawing dating from the second half of the 16th c. showing the old façade of the Duomo (on the right of the entrance).

Donatello's cantoria

Among the most interesting works are: along the wall left of the entrance the statue of St Luke (by Nanni di Banco), the statue of John the Evangelist (by Donatello) and the statue of St Matthew (by Bernardo Ciuffagni); along the left-hand wall the statue of Pope Boniface VIII (by Arnolfo di Cambio). On the wall opposite the entrance the statue of "S. Reparata", the statue of the "Madonna and Child" and the statue of the "Madonna of the Nativity" (all by Arnolfo di Cambio).

On the right-hand wall the statue "The Virgin interred in the Sepulchre" (plaster cast; by Arnolfo di Cambio) and the statues of St Augustine and St Gregory (by Niccolò di Piero Lamberti).

In the "Small Room" are missals (damaged by the 1966 floods), precious reliquaries and other items of gold and silver from the cathedral treasury.   Small room

Also of interest is the original wooden model for the lantern of the cathedral with Brunelleschi's signature in his own hand.

Goldsmiths' octagon
This contains relics from the period 1300–1800.

On the mezzanine is Michelangelo's "Pietà".   Mezzanine

Sala delle Cantorie   First floor
The "Room of the Cantoria" contains the two marble choir-gallery parapets or cantoria which used to support the console of the cathedral organ. Until 1686 they stood below the dome and were dismantled on the occasion of the wedding of Grand Duke Cosimo III and Violante Beatrice of Bavaria.

To the left of the entrance is the Cantoria by Luca della Robbia (1431–8), while opposite is the Cantoria by Donatello. The famous wooden figure of "Mary Magdalene" by Donatello, which was brought here from the Battistero (see entry) is under Donatello's choral gallery.

Against the left-hand wall are the statues of John the Baptist (1423–7) and Habakkuk, popularly known as "Lo Zuccone", i.e. Baldhead (1434–6), both by Donatello.

To the right of the entrance is Donatello's sculpture of Abraham and Isaac (1421).

Sala delle Formelle del Campanile di Giotto

This room contains the bas-reliefs which formerly decorated the panels on the lower storey of Giotto's Campanile (see Duomo Santa Maria del Fiore, Campanile); these were replaced by copies between 1965 and 1967. The panels with the allegorical figures are by Andrea Pisano (first two bottom panels on the long right-hand wall, bottom row on right-hand wall opposite, bottom row on the long left-hand wall, bottom row on left-hand wall opposite), Luca della Robbia (bottom row on the long right-hand wall), by artists of the school of Pisano (top row on the right-hand wall opposite, top row on the long left-hand wall, top row on the left-hand wall opposite) and Alberto Arnoldi (top row, long right-hand wall).

Sala dell'Altare

The greatest treasures of the Altar Room are the silk and gold needlework panels with scenes from the life of St John the Baptist, from designs by Antonio Pollaiolo (long left-hand wall) and the silver altar of the Battistero (left-hand wall opposite), one of the finest examples of the art of the Florentine silversmiths. It was begun in the Gothic style in 1366 and completed during the Renaissance (1480). The altar is decorated with prophets and sibyls, scenes from the life of John the Baptist and other scenes from the scriptures.

The other works in the room are by 14th and 15th c. artists (including Giovanni della Robbia, Tino da Camaino, Giovanni di Balduccio, Giovanni Bandini and Andrea Pisano).

Michelangelo's Pietà

Since 1981 one of the most famous sculptures of Western art has been kept in the cathedral museum – Michelangelo's Pietà, the marble group created by the artist in his old age but never completed. The limp, broken figure of the lifeless Christ, the face of Mary with only a hint of her suffering, the grief-stricken visage of Nicodemus, possibly a self-portrait, the unfulfilled nature of the whole group (the figure of Mary Magdalene on the left was added later) – all this combines in an incomparable expression of the concept of death and man's helplessness in the face of mortality. Michelangelo smashed this statue because he was not satisfied with his own work. His pupil Calcagni reassembled the fragments and, except for the figure of Christ, added the finishing touches.

Museo dell'Opera di Santa Croce

See Santa Croce

Museo di San Marco

See San Marco

Museo Stibbert: housed in the Villa Montughi

Museo Stibbert (Stibbert Museum)

From 1860 onwards the Scottish officer Frederick Stibbert collected art treasures in the Villa Montughi just outside the city. In 1906 he gave them to the city of Florence.

The collection of arms is especially interesting; in the huge "Cavalcade Room" is a row of horsemen with uniforms and weapons from various countries, and further exhibits – furniture, paintings, textiles and other works of artistic value – show the feeling for art and the taste of the collector.

Location
Via Frederico Stibbert 26

Bus
1

Opening times
Mon.–Wed., Fri., Sat. 9 a.m.–2 p.m.; Sun. and public holidays 9 a.m.–1 p.m.

Museo di Firenze com'era – Museo Storico Topografico   K5
(Florence as it used to be – Historical Museum)

In the old convent of the Oblates with its fine 15th c. cloister can be found a collection of paintings, drawings, prints and photographs that show how the city of Florence has developed since the end of the 15th c.
It also shows the everyday life of the people of Florence, their various festivals and their great processions.
The museum is open on weekdays (except Thursdays) from 9 a.m. to 2 p.m. and on Sundays and public holidays from 8 a.m. to 1 p.m.

Location
Via dell'Oriuolo 24 (opposite Santa Maria Nuova)

Buses
4, 9, 14, 17, 19, 22, 23, 36, 37

Museo Zoologico "La Specola" (Zoological Museum)   H7

Location
Via Romana 17

Bus
B

The Zoological Museum is in the Palazzo Torrigiani, also known as "La Specola" i.e. "the observatory", because Grand Duke Pietro Leopoldo built an astronomical and meteorological observatory here in 1775.

The museum's collection of anatomical specimens in wax is particularly interesting.

The museum is open on Tuesdays from 9 a.m. to 12.30 p.m. and on Sundays from 9 a.m. to noon. The anatomical department can be visited on Saturdays between 4 and 6 p.m. (4–5 p.m. in winter). The museum is closed from 20 July to 15 August.

Museum of the History of Science

See Palazzo Castellanti

*Ognissanti (All Saints' Church)   H5

Location
Piazza Ognissanti

Buses
6, 9, 11, 36

The church of "Ognissanti" (All Saints), one of the first Baroque churches in Florence, dates back to a 13th c. building but was completely renovated in the 16th and 17th c. Restoration work had to be carried out in 1872 and after the severe flooding in 1966.

The main features of the exterior are the terracotta "Coronation of the Virgin with Saints", ascribed to both Giovanni della Robbia and Benedetto Buglioni, and the Romanesque Campanile.

Of interest in the interior:
At the second altar on the right there is Domenico Ghirlandaio's "Madonna della Misericordia" ("Madonna of the Protecting Cloak", 1470) and a fresco with a Pietà by Domenico and Davide Ghirlandaio (1472).

Sacristy
The sacristy contains a painting on wood of "Christ Crucified" in the style of Giotto and a fresco of the Crucifixion by Taddeo Gaddi.

Cloister of the old monastery
Entered through the transept or from the square. It consists of Ionic columns. The frescoes with scenes from the "Life of St Francis" (17th c.) are currently being restored.

Refectory
Famous frescoes are also to be found in the refectory: Domenico Ghirlandaio's "Last Supper" and "St Jerome in his Study" (1480) as well as Sandro Botticelli's famous "Saint Augustine in his Chamber".

Opificio e Museo delle Pietre Dure   K5
(Mosaic Workshops and Museum)

Location
Via degli Alfani 78

The so-called "Florentine mosaic", semi-precious stones inlaid in stone, has a long and unique tradition. Skilled craftsmen

were especially in demand for the princes' chapel of San Lorenzo (see entry) in 1588. They started up in shops in the Palazzo degli Uffizi (see entry) and then after 1796 moved to the Convent of San Niccolò where this special Florentine craft is still carried on today.
Also to be found here is a museum full of interesting examples of the art of these consummate craftsmen.

Buses
B, 4, 11, 17

Opening times
Mon.–Sat. 9 a.m.–1 p.m.

** Orsanmichele (San Michele in Orto; Church)   J6

The present church, a very well-preserved 14th c. building, developed from an oratory (Or San Michele is the abbreviated form of San Michele in Orto) and granary. These housed a miraculous picture that came to attract more worshippers than buyers. As a result the building's religious function was given precedence at the end of the 14th c.
The delicate articulation of the external walls, its ornamentation, arches, niches, figures, mouldings, the marble infill in the window openings and the uncluttered tracery of the pillared arcades raise the church high in the architectural rankings.
The beauty of the architecture is complemented by important works of sculpture.

Location
Via Arte della Lana 1

Buses
B, 6, 11, 14, 19, 23, 31, 32

Opening times
8 a.m.–noon, 2–7 p.m. daily

The painstakingly and artistically wrought niches (or tabernacles) on the façade, commissioned by the individual guilds in the city, contain the guilds' patron saints.

Exterior

On the Via dei Calzaiuoli side:
Left Lorenzo Ghiberti's "St John the Baptist" (1414), the first major Renaissance bronze statue; in the next niche (by Donatello) "Incredulity of St Thomas", a major work by Andrea del Verrocchio (c. 1480); right "St Luke" by Giambologna (1600).

On the Via dei Lamberti (S) side:
"St Mark", an early work by Donatello (1411); "St James" by Lamberti (c. 1422); "Madonna delle Rose" (1399, probably by Piero di Giovanni Tedesco) and "St John the Evangelist" by Baccio da Montelupo (1515).

W façade
"St Matthew", Lorenzo Ghiberti's most important large statue (1419–22), "St Stephen", also by Ghiberti (1428), and Nanni di Banco's "St Eligius" (1415).

N side
"St Peter" (1408–13) attributed to Donatello. "St Philip" (1415) and "Four Crowned Saints" (1408), a group of four martyrs, both works by Nanni di Banco, and Donatello's "St George" (1418; copy, original in the Museo Nazionale del Bargello, see Palazzo del Bargello).

The interior of the two-naved church is impressive on account of its frescoes, paintings and stained-glass windows.

Interior

In the left-hand nave is the altar of St Anne with Francesco da Sangallo's marble sculpture "Madonna and Child with St Anne" (1526).

At the back of the right-hand nave is Orcagna's famous Gothic marble tabernacle (1349–59), the rich ornamentation of which sets off the miraculous picture of the Madonna (by Bernardo Daddi, 1347). Reliefs on the plinth show scenes from the life of the Virgin (front) and "Death and Assumption of the Virgin" with a self-portrait of Orcagna (back; 1359).

The tabernacle is decorated with angels and prophets, sibyls, apostles and allegorical figures of the virtues. Pietro Migliore's marble grille with a bronze trellis (1366) is also an interesting feature.

Opposite Orsanmichele is the small but interesting church of San Carlo dei Lombardi (see entry).

Orti Oricellari (Oricellari Gardens)   H5

Location
Via degli Orti Oricellari

Buses
A, 4, 9, 13, 14, 17, 22, 23, 26, 27, 28, 29, 30, 35

Adjacent to the Palazzo Venturi-Ginori is part of the famous Orti Oricellari. To this garden Bernardo Rucellai transferred the Accademia Platonica (Philosophers' Academy) in 1498. The Academy was visited by Pope Leo X (1516) and Emperor Charles V (1530).
In the centre of the garden is a colossal statue of Polyphemus (8·4 m – 27·6 ft high) by Antonio Novelli, a pupil of Giambologna.

Orto Botanico (Botanical garden; officially: Giardino dei Semplici)   K4/5

Location
Via la Pira 4

Buses
4, 6, 7, 10, 11, 17, 20

The "Giardino dei Semplici" was founded in 1545 by Cosimo I for the study of exotic plants. It is the headquarters of the Italian Botanical Society, the "Società Botanica Italiana", and together with the school and the museum forms part of the "Institute of Botany".
The museum is open on Mondays, Wednesdays and Fridays from 9 a.m. until midday.

Palazzo Altoviti-Valori   K6

Location
Borgo degli Albizi 18

Buses
13, 14, 19, 23, 31, 32

The Palazzo Altoviti in Borgo degli Albizi, a street with many fine town houses, first belonged to the Albizi family and then to the Valori and Guicciardini families.
In the 16th c. Baccio Valòri decorated it with busts of famous Florentines (Ficino, Vespucci, Alberti, Guicciardini, Dante, Petrarch, Boccaccio and others) which is why it became disrespectfully known by the locals as "the Rogues' Gallery".

Palazzo Antinori   J5

Location
Piazza Antinori 3

Buses
A, 1, 6, 7, 10, 22, 25

In Piazza Antinori, opposite the church of San Gaetano, is the town house of the Antinori family. The severe and elegant palace was built between 1461 and 1466 in the style of Giuliano da Maiano.
For many generations the Antinoris have devoted themselves to the production of good wine. (There is a wine bar in the palace.)

Palazzo Arcivescovile (Archbishop's Palace)   J5

The Archbishop's Palace was built between 1573 and 1584 by
Giovanni Antonio Dosio for Cardinal Alessandro Medici who
later became Pope Leo XI, but it was not finally completed until
1735, by Ciurini. During this long period it developed into a
mixture of medieval and "modern" elements. In 1895 the
whole palace was moved back 50 yards to make room for the
city's growing traffic.

Location
Piazza San Giovanni

Buses
1, 6, 7, 10, 11, 13, 14, 17,
19, 23, 25, 31, 32, 33

Palazzo dell'Arte della Lana   J6

Florence prospered in the Middle Ages by producing and
processing wool and selling the finished products. This is
evident in the palace of the guild of weavers and wool
merchants which had 200 shops and employed 30,000
workmen. The irregular palace complex, linked to the church of
Orsanmichele (see entry) by a bridge (built in 1569 by
Buontalenti), was begun in 1308. After it was restored in 1905
it became the headquarters of the Dante Society. Today the
palace houses a shop, and cross vaults can be seen in its
showrooms.
A bridge gives access to the interior rooms, the Saloni di
Orsanmichele, which contain fine paintings (Taddeo Gaddi's
"Entombment"). On the corner of Via dell'Arte della Lana and
Via Orsanmichele is the 14th c. Gothic tabernacle of Santa
Maria della Tromba.

Location
Via dell'Arte della Lana

Buses
B, 6, 11

**Palazzo del Bargello e Museo Nazionale   K6
(Bargello Palace and National Museum)

The huge bulk of the sturdy tower and crenellated walls of the
Bargello, the massive palace which the citizens of Florence
built after 1250 as testimony to their victory over the nobility, is
one of the city's landmarks. Located in Piazza San Firenze,
between Via del Proconsolo, Via della Vigna Vecchia, Via
dell'Acqua and Via Ghibellina, nowadays it houses the
National Museum (photo on p. 65).
In 1261 it became the seat of the Podestà, the governing body
of the city. After 1502 this was the site of the Rota
(ecclesiastical court) and prison and in 1574 the palace
became the seat of the Bargello (chief constable). In 1859
Italy's first national museum and most important collection of
sculpture (apart from those in the Vatican) was installed in the
palace.

Location
Via del Proconsolo

Buses
13, 14, 19, 23, 31, 32

Opening times
Tues.–Sat 9 a.m.–2 p.m.,
Sun. and public holidays
9 a.m.–1 p.m.

Closed
Mon.

**Museo Nazionale del Bargello (National Museum)

The National Museum contains works by important 14th–
16th c. Tuscan sculptors (especially Donatello, della Robbia
and Michelangelo).

Courtyard
The courtyard is worth visiting for its architecture alone. It is
surrounded on three sides by an arcade (round arches,

Opening times
Tues.–Sat. 9 a.m.–2 p.m.;
Sun. and public holidays
9 a.m.–1 p.m.

Ground floor

Palazzo del Bargello

octagonal columns, groin vaulting). On the fourth side an open staircase leads to the upper floors.

Pillars and walls are decorated with the coats of arms of the Podestà, the members of the Rota and the quarters and boroughs of the city. In the centre of the courtyard is an octagonal pillar. Nearby is where the scaffold used to stand when the Bargello was also a prison.

Today the courtyard and arcade are used for the display of sculpture. There are works on view by Niccolò di Piero Lamberti, Vincenzo Danti, Cosimo Cenni, Vincenzo Gemito, Bartolomeo Ammannati, Domenico Poggini and Giambologna.

Michelangelo Room

The courtyard leads into the rooms containing works by Michelangelo: "Brutus", a marble statue (c. 1540); "Madonna and Child with the young John the Baptist", a circular relief, carved for Bartolomeo Pitti about 1504; "David" (c. 1531), also known as "Little Apollo"; "Drunken Bacchus", Michelangelo's first large sculpture (1497–9).

Other works are by 16th c. artists. Worthy of particular mention are Jacopo Sansovino's statue of Bacchus (c. 1520), the bronze bust of Michelangelo by Daniele da Volterra, the bust of Cosino I by Benvenuto Cellini (1557) and other of Cellini's works, including his marble statue of Narcissus (1540).

First Floor

Loggia

The Loggia on the first floor has Giambologna's bronze statue of Mercury (1564), his important allegory of "Architecture", and sculptures by Baccio Bandinelli and Francesco Moschino.

Grand Hall

This contains statues by Donatello, including his "St George" (1416, marble statue formerly in a niche in the church of Orsanmichele), "Marble David" (1408–9), "Bronze David" (made in 1430 for Cosimo the Elder), "St John as a Child" (Casa Martelli) and the "Marzocco Lion" (1420). Other artists represented in this room are Desiderio da Settignano, Vecchietta, Luca della Robbia and Bertoldo di Giovanni. Filippo Brunelleschi's and Lorenzo Ghiberti's models for the competition for the N portal of the Battistero (see entry) complete the display.

Also on display on the first floor are frescoes in the Chapel of the Podestà, ivory carvings (Ivory Room), a collection of majolica (Majolica Room) and the work of enamellers and goldsmiths (Room of the Goldsmiths).

Second floor

Verrocchio Room

As its name implies, this room chiefly contains works by Verrocchio, including his "Noblewoman", "David" (bronze), "Madonna and Child" (high relief) and "Resurrection of Christ" (high relief).

Other artists represented in this room are Antonio Rossellino, Mino da Fiesole, Antonio del Pollaiolo, Francesco Laurana and Matteo Civitati.

Characteristic features of the Palazzo del Bargello: its sturdy tower and its crenellations ▶

Palazzo del Bargello

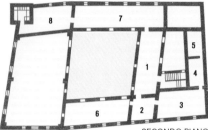

SECONDO PIANO

Palazzo del Bargello

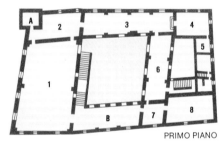

PRIMO PIANO

Museo Nazionale

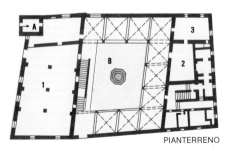

PIANTERRENO

SECOND FLOOR (SECONDO PIANO)
1 Sala di G. della Robbia
  Glazed terracottas, by Della
  Robbia, plus works by Rustici,
  Bandinelli, Giambologna
2 Sala di A. della Robbia
3 Sala del Verrocchio
  Busts and reliefs, by Verrocchio
  and others
4, 5 Medici collection of coins
  and medals
6 Sala del Camino
  Small bronze figures
7 Sala delle Armi
  Collection of weapons
8 Sala della Torre
  Tapestries, textiles

FIRST FLOOR (PRIMO PIANO)
A Tower
B Loggia
  "Mercury" and "Allegory of
  Architecture", by Giambologna.
  Works by 15th and 16th c.
  Florentine artists
1 Salone del Consiglio
  Generale or Salone di
  Donatello
  "San Giorgio", "San
  Giovannino", "David", "Il
  Marzocco", by Donatello, "Il
  Sacrificio di Isacco", by
  Brunelleschi. Works by L. della
  Robbia, Ghiberti, Michelozzo
2 Sala della Torre
  Tapestries, etc. from Germany
  and Asia Minor (15th and
  16th c.)
3 Salone del Podestà
  Enamels and goldsmiths' work
4 Cappella del Podestà
  Frescoes, probably by Giotto
5 Sagrestia
  Frescoes (14th c.)
6 Sala degli Avori
  Wood carvings (14th and
  16th c.), ivory carvings
7 Sala delle Oreficerie
  Jewellery, coins, enamels, silver
  goblets
8 Sala delle Maioliche
  Majolica (15th and 16th c.)

GROUND FLOOR (PIANTERRENO)
A Entrance and vestibule
B Courtyard with octagonal
  fountain
1 Michelangelo Room
  "David" (c 1531), "Brutus"
  (1540), "Drunken Bacchus"
  (c. 1498), by Michelangelo
  "Bacchus", by Sansovino
  Bust of Cosimo I, by Cellini
  Costanza Bonarelli, by Bernini
2 Gothic sculpture room
3 14th c. Florentine
  sculpture, inc. works by T.
  di Camaino, A. Arnoldi, S.
  Talenti, Arnolfo di Cambio

Great Hall: statues by Donatello

Andrea Robbia Room
Glazed terracottas by this artist.

Giovanni della Robbia Room
Glazed terracottas by Giovanni della Robbia.

Coin collection
Two rooms contain the famous Medici coin collection that was started by Lorenzo de' Medici and constantly added to by his successors.

Also on display on the second floor are tapestries and textiles from Florence (Tower Room), 13th–17th c. weapons (Armoury) and a collection of small bronze figures (Fireplace Room).

Palazzo Bartolini Salimbeni   J6

This palace was built between 1517 and 1520 by Baccio d'Agnolo and thoroughly restored in 1962. The people of Florence reproached the architect with having used too many Roman elements (the Classical forms of Bramante and Raphael) more suited to a church than to a town house. The architect responded by inscribing above the portal "carpere promptius quam imitari" ("it is easier to carp than to imitate"). Another inscription above the windows gives the clue to the secret of the success of the former occupants: "Per non dormire" ("By not sleeping").

Location
Piazza S. Trinità

Buses
A, 6, 11

Palazzo dei Capitani di Parte Guelfa (Or Palazzo di Parte Guelfa)   J6

Location
Piazza de Parte Guelfa

Bus
B

The palace's Gothic windows, the covered open staircase and the merlons hark back to the 14th c. In the power struggle between the Guelphs and the Ghibellines, i.e. the supporters of the Pope and of the Holy Roman Emperor, that engulfed the towns and cities of Italy in the 13th c., this house is where the Capitani di Parte Guelfa held in trust the property confiscated from the defeated Ghibellines.

The 15th c. alterations were directed by the architects Brunelleschi and Francesco della Luna.

The medieval palace contains splendid rooms with harmonious proportions. The ceilings and walls were decorated by Giambologna, Luca della Robbia, Donatello and others.

Today the palace houses the head offices of various organisations.

Palazzo Castellani con Museo di Storia della Scienza   J6
(Museum of the History of Science)

Location
Piazza dei Giudici 1

Buses
13n, 19n, 31, 32, 33

Opening times
10 a.m.–1 p.m., 2–4 p.m. daily; Sun. and public holidays 10 a.m.–1 p.m.

Closed
last Sun in the month, every Sun. in July and August

From 1574 to 1841 this severe medieval building that looks like a fort was the headquarters of the Rota court (hence the name of the square, "Giudici"=judges). Since 1930 the palace has housed the Museum of the History of the Experimental Sciences. It was seriously damaged in the 1966 floods.

In the collection are instruments and scientific objects, some belonging to the Medici and some from other Florentine institutes: optical and mathematical apparatus, including a mechanical writing device, electrical apparatus, instruments for astronomy and cosmography and physical and anatomical models.

One room is devoted to Galileo and his discoveries.

Palazzo Corsini con Galleria Corsini (Art Gallery)   H6

Location
Lungarno Corsini 10
(entrance Via di Parione 11)

Buses
A, 6, 11, 36, 37

The Palazzo Corsini stands beside the Arno, and its impressive façade is best viewed from the opposite bank (it is incomplete; the left-hand wing that should offset the right-hand wing is missing).

The palace, still owned by the Corsini family, was built by Pier Francesco Silvani and Antonio Ferri (1648–56) in the 16th c. style but also with occasional Baroque elements. The spiral staircase inside the palace is one of the most important examples of Baroque architecture in Florence.

The palace houses the most important private collection in Florence (on the first floor), founded in 1765 by Lorenzo Corsini, a nephew of Pope Clement XII. Unlike other museums the pictures are not arranged chronologically but in accordance with the old criterion of decoration and symmetry. A painting should be part of the decoration of the room and not be looked at for its own sake.

On display are fine examples of the Italian and foreign schools of the 17th c. and of 15th and 16th c. Florentine painting (including Raphael).

There are several statues and busts of Pope Clement XII (1730–40) who was a member of the Corsini family.

Palazzo Corsini: view from the opposite bank of the Arno

*Palazzo Davanzati con Museo dell'Antica Casa Fiorentina J6
(Museum of the Old Florentine House)

The severe five-storey façade of the Palazzo Davanzati is divided up on the ground floor by three massive doors, topped by a loggia and decorated in the centre by a splendid coat of arms of the Davanzati family (in summer the curtains are fastened to the iron bars in front of the windows).

The Davizzi built a town house here in 1300; one of the family was Gonfaloniere of the Republic in 1294. In the 16th c. the palace was acquired by the Bartolini family and later (1578) by the Davanzati. In 1906 the building was bought by the art dealer Elia Volpi and restored to its former glory. Since 1956 it has contained the "Museum of the Old Florentine House".

Location
Piazza Davanzati

Buses
B, 6, 11, 36, 37

Museo dell'Antica Casa Fiorentina

The "Museum of the Old Florentine House" covers three floors and contains furniture, drawings, sculptures, tapestries, ceramics, textiles and everyday objects from the Middle Ages, the Renaissance and the Baroque period.

The "Parrot Room" on the first floor is especially interesting. It gets its name from its decoration. The walls are painted to look like tapestries with parrots. The room has a painted wooden ceiling.

The exhibits have been assembled from the Museo Nazionale del Bargello (see Palazzo del Bargello), other collections in Florence and from gifts. They provide a glimpse of the highly-cultivated life of the citizens of Florence who furnished their houses with valuable art treasures and utensils.

Opening times
Tues.–Sat. 9 a.m.–2 p.m.;
Sun. and public holidays
9 a.m.–1 p.m.

Closed
Mon.

Guided tours
9, 10, 11 a.m., noon, 1 p.m.

69

Palazzo Frescobaldi H/J6

Location
Piazza Frescobaldi 1

Buses
A, B

In the Piazza Frescobaldi, on the left bank of the Arno at the end of the Ponte Santa Trinità (see entry), stands the palace of the Frescobaldi family. Built in the 13th c., it was used by Charles de Valois, the brother of the French king, as his residence when his peace mission on behalf of Pope Boniface VIII brought him to Florence in 1301 (one of the consequences of his meditation was Dante's being sent into exile).

Next to it is the Baroque Palazzo dei Padri delle Missioni, today an Istituto Magistrale.

*Palazzo Gondi K6

Location
Piazza San Firenze 1

Buses
B, 19n, 23, 31, 32, 33

The Palazzo Gondi, one of the finest examples of 15th c. Florentine palaces, was built between 1490 and 1501 by Giuliano da Sangallo but not completed until 1874 by Poggi. The main feature of its façade is the way the stone has been meticulously worked on the individual storeys, becoming flatter towards the top.

The courtyard, one of the most charming of the Renaissance, is especially worth seeing. Here again one is struck by the careful use of the material and the artistic craftsmanship (on the capitals, the staircase and the fountain).

Palazzo Grifoni

See Palazzo Riccardi-Manelli

Palazzo Guadagni H6/7

Location
Piazza di Santo Spirito 10

Bus
B

The Palazzo in Piazza di Santo Spirito has a classical severity and beauty. Simone del Pollaiolo, known as Cronaca, built it (probably 1503–6) for Riniero Dei. The three storeys, in different styles, are topped by an open loggia.

In 1684 it was acquired by the Marchese Guadagni and later by the Dufour-Berte family.

**Palazzo Medici-Riccardi e Museo Mediceo (Medici Museum) J5

Location
Via Cavour 1 (Via Larga)/Via Gori

Buses
1, 4, 6, 7, 10, 11, 17, 25

The majestic bulk of the Palazzo Medici, opposite the church of San Lorenzo (see entry), bespeaks the power of a ruling dynasty. At the same time its limitation to the bare essentials testifies to the wise lack of ostentation of the Medici family at that time. They presided over a democratic-republican community and would never have chosen to behave like monarchs of the city.

The palace was built between 1444 and 1464 by Michelozzo for Cosimo the Elder. All the Medici princes lived and ruled here

Palazzo Medici-Riccardi: built for Cosimo the Elder ▶

Palazzo Medici-Riccardi

until Cosimo I (1540) moved into the Palazzo Vecchio (see entry). In 1655 it was acquired by the Riccardi family who enlarged it by extending the side of the palace; in 1818 it was bought by the Grand Dukes of Tuscany. Today it houses the Medici Museum (ground floor) and the Prefecture (first floor). Its valuable art treasures and furnishings have been severely depleted through being plundered, destroyed or sold off.

Exterior

An interesting feature of the façade is that each of the three storeys is very different from the others. The windows on the ground floor are supported on brackets and therefore seem to be "kneeling". they are surmounted by wide arches and every other one has a triangular gable. The windows on the first floor have beautiful decoration, while the second floor is dominated by a heavy cornice.

On the corner opposite San Lorenzo (see entry) is the Medici coat of arms (six balls, the top one decorated with a lily).

Interior

The interior of the palace was altered by the Riccardi family, and there are only a few of the original Medici rooms – on the ground floor, where the Medici Museum is, and on the first floor.

The archway leads into the square courtyard, with twelve marble medallions above the colonnade and the statue of Orpheus by Baccio Bandinelli, then comes the smaller garden courtyard.

The entrance to the Medici Museum, which opened in 1929, is in the main courtyard. The most interesting room on the first floor is the chapel, built by Michelozzo and covered in frescoes. The wall frescoes – "The Procession of the Magi to Bethlehem" – constitute one of the principal works of Benozzo Gozzoli.

Gozzoli incorporated two historical events into his cycle of frescoes: the magnificent assembly of bishops which took place in Florence in 1439 and which led to the union of the Roman and Greek churches, and the visit of Pope Pius II, the great humanist Aeneas Silvius Piccolomini, to Florence in 1459. There are portraits of some of the people who took part in these events including Joseph, the Patriarch of Constantinople (as the oldest of the Magi), John VI, Emperor in the East, and Lorenzo de' Medici (as a young boy).

The frescoes are very well preserved and with their bright colours present a vivid and lively picture of Florence in the 15th c. and the culture and prosperity of the Renaissance.

The altarpiece is a copy of Filippo Lippi's famous "Nativity".

In the Galleria di Luca Giordano is the "Apotheosis of the Second Medici Dynasty", an important fresco by Luca Giordano (1682–3).

The Galleria leads to the Biblioteca Riccardiana e Moreniana. It is worth having a look at the exhibition room: the vaulted ceiling is painted with frescoes by Luca Giordano (1683) on the allegorical theme of Intellect aiding Man to free himself from Enslavement by Stupidity.

Museo Mediceo (Medici Museum)

The Medici Museum, containing the works of art and furnishings acquired or owned by the Medici, keeps alive the memory of the great dynasty that made Florence one of the most famed cities of art in the West. A brief mention of some of the main exhibits is given below, with a recommendation to look at the unsullied architecture and tasteful décor of the rooms themselves.

Of especial interest: "Madonna and Child", one of Filippo Lippi's most important works (1442), the death-mask of Lorenzo the Magnificent, and a painting by Jacopo da Empolo, "The Wedding of Catherine de' Medici and Henri IV of France" (1533).

Opening times
Mon., Tues., Thurs.–Sat.
9 a.m.–noon, 3–5 p.m.;
Sun. and public holidays
9 a.m.–12.30 p.m.

Closed
Wed.

Palazzo Nonfinito   K6
(Museo Nazionale di Antropologia ed Etnologia; Museum of Mankind)

The Palazzo Nonfinito is, as its name suggests, unfinished, a fact belied by its exterior. Allessandro Strozzi commissioned the architect Bernardo Buontalenti to build a new town house for his family near the Palazzo Pazzi (see entry). Neither Buontalenti nor his successors, however, were able to complete the large building with the beautiful inner courtyard. Since 1869 the Palazzo has housed the Museo Nazionale di Antropologia ed Etnologia (Museum of Mankind) with anthropological and ethnological collections from all over the world.

Location
Via del Proconsolo 12

Buses
14, 19n, 23, 31, 32, 33

Opening times
Mon., Wed., Fri.
9 a.m.–1 p.m.

Palazzo Pandolfini   K4

The famous painter Raphael designed a palace for Giannozzo Pandolfini, the Bishop of Troia, and Giovanni Francesco and Aristotile da Sangallo put his plans into effect about 1520.

The charm of the palace lies in its simple elegance and the perfect expression of elements of the Roman Renaissance. It was originally intended to extend the palace to the right so that the portal would have been in the middle. However under Pope Clement VII, a Medici – his name can be seen next to that of Leo X on the right-hand side – it was obviously decided to leave the building half-finished.

Location
Via San Gallo 74

Buses
B, 20, 34

Palazzo dei Pazzi   K6

The palace was built for Jacopo de' Pazzi who was executed in 1478 after the conspiracy against Lorenzo and Giuliano de' Medici. The work was originally under the direction of Brunelleschi (1430) but was later taken over by Giuliano da Maiano (1462–72) whose contribution is marked by its meticulous execution and love for architectural detail.

The Pazzi family, who moved to Florence from Fiesole (see entry) in the Middle Ages, personified commercial acumen and hunger for power. Once Lorenzo de' Medici had survived their murder bid their attempt to break the power of the Medicis was doomed to failure. The family was banned and their palace was handed over to the Cibo family and later belonged to the Strozzis and Quarantesis.

Location
Via del Proconsolo 10,
Borgo degli Albizi

Buses
13r, 14, 19n, 23, 31, 32, 33

Palazzo Pitti and Museums H/J6/7

Location
Piazza Pitti

Bus
B

Opening times
Tues.–Sat. 9 a.m.–2 p.m.;
Sun. and public holidays
9 a.m.–1 p.m.

Closed
Mon.

The Palazzo Pitti ranks as Florence's most important palace together with the Palazzo Vecchio (they are joined together by a passage) and the Palazzo Medici-Riccardi (see entries). Its size is impressive – it covers a surface area of 344,320 sq. ft (32,000 sq. m) and its façade is 224 yd (205 m) across and 118 ft (36 m) high at the centre – and so is its architecture, an effect that is heightened by the way the square fronting it slopes slightly uphill towards it.

The art gallery (Galleria Palatina or Pitti) in the Palazzo Pitti is one of the most important in the world, almost on equal terms, so far as works of art are concerned, with the collections of the Uffizi (see Palazzo e Galleria degli Uffizi). The palace also houses the Museo degli Argenti (Silver Museum), the Galleria d'Arte Moderna (Gallery of Modern Art), the Contini Bonacassi collection, the Museo delle Carrozze (Carriage Museum) and the Appartamenti ex Reali (Royal Apartments).

Palazzo Pitti

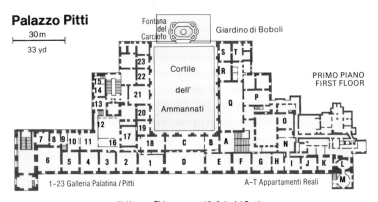

1 Sala di Venere
  Titian, Tintoretto
2 Sala di Apollo
  Van Dyck, Rubens,
  Reni, del Sarto,
  Titian, Tintoretto
3 Sala di Marte
  Tintoretto, Reni,
  Titian, Rubens,
  Murillo, Veronese
4 Sala di Giove
  Raphael, Bordone,
  Rubens, del Sarto,
  Perugino, Guercino
5 Sala di Saturno
  Raphael ("Madonna
  della Seggiola")
6 Sala dell'Iliade

Velázquez, Titian,
Raphael
7 Sala della Stufa
  Frescoes by Rosselli,
  da Cortona
8 Sala dell'Educazione
  di Giove
  Caravaggio, Allori
9 Saletta da Bagno
10 Sala di Ulisse
  Raphael, Reni, Lippi
11 Sala di Prometeo
  Signorelli, Lippi
12 Corridoio delle
  Colonne
13 Sala della Giustizia
  Veronese, Titian
14 Sala di Flora
  Canova, Bronzino

15 Sala dei Putti
  Jordaens, Rubens
16 Galleria Poccetti
  Pontormo, Rubens,
  Ribera, Dughet
17 Sala della Musica
18 Sala Castognoli
19 Sala delle Allegorie
20 Sala delle Belle Arti
21 Salone d'Ercole
22 Sala dell'Aurora
23 Sala di Berenice

A Vestibolo
B Sala degli Staffieri
C Galleria delle Statue
D Sala delle Nicchie
E Sala verde
F Sala del trono

G Sala celeste
H Cappella
I Sala dei pappagalli
J Sala gialla
K Camera da letto
L Gabinetto da
  toletta
M Sala da musica
  e da lavoro
N Camera da letto
O Salotto di
  ricevimento
P Sala di Bona
Q Sala da ballo
R Sala della Fede
S Sala della Carità
T Sala della Giustizia

Palazzo Pitti: home of some of Florence's major museums

The various museums in the Palazzo Pitti have been undergoing reorganisation since 1970 so there may be some discrepancies in the listing of the exhibits.

A respected and wealthy Florentine merchant family, the Pittis were on a par with the Medicis when it came to pride and ambition. Consequently in 1447 Luca Pitti laid plans for a magnificent palace on the left bank of the Arno a little above the town. The architect Luca Fancelli was in charge of the preliminary work (1457–66), possibly based on designs by Brunelleschi. Between 1558 and 1570 Eleonora of Toledo, the wife of Cosimo I, who had acquired the palace in 1549, had it completely renovated and considerably enlarged by Bartolomeo Ammanati, who was followed by other architects, interior designers and artists.

The new owners, the Medici, and Cosimo III in particular, purchased valuable pictures to decorate the apartments. These form the basis of the Galleria Palatina. Classical and contemporary statues were also added.

The Palazzo Pitti became the residence of the country's rulers (1864–71) when Florence was the capital of a partially united Italy. In 1919 King Victor Emanuel III finally gave it to the city, which had the various museums enlarged.

Architecture at its most creative can be seen in the façade of the palace with its massive ashlar stonework, high-vaulted windows and stepped storeys, and in the Rondò di Bacco, the courtyard laid out in the Mannerist way by Ammanati (1558–70), looking like a grotto enlivened by "rustication". Adjoining it is the terrace of the Boboli Gardens (see Giardino di Boboli) with its fountain and statues.

Palazzo Pitti

Filippo Lippi:
"Madonna and Child"

Raphael:
"Madonna della Seggiola"

Raphael:
"Madonna del Granduca"

Galleria Palatina/Galleria Pitti

Opening times
Tues.–Sat. 9 a.m.–2 p.m.,
Sun. and public holidays
9 a.m.–1 p.m.

Closed
Mon.

The entrance to the palace leads past the Cappella Palatina (completely covered in frescoes) to the Galleria Palatina or Galleria Pitti (first floor), where the paintings are not in chronological order but are arranged as part of the décor as an adjunct to the state-rooms and their costly furnishings.

The collection was begun about 1620 by Cosimo II and finally made accessible to the public by the Italian kings.

The rooms are named after the themes of the pictures they contain or the artists being represented.

Especially interesting are the works of Raphael (1483–1520), Andrea del Sarto (1486–1530), Titian (1490–1576), Tintoretto (1518–94) and Rubens (1577–1640).

The Sala di Venere containing the first paintings is reached from the staircase via the vestibule, the Sala degli Staffieri, the Galleria delle Statue and the Galleria delle Nicchie.

Sala di Venere
Among the most important paintings in the "Venus Room" are the Pietro da Cortona ceiling, "Return of the Hunters" (Sustermans), "The Portrait of a Lady" (Titian), "Pietro Aretino" (Titian), "Return from the Hayfields" and "Ulysses in the Phaecian Isle" (Rubens), "Concert" (Titian) and "Seascape at Sunset" (Salvatore Rosa).

Peter Paul Rubens: "Holy Family"

Titian: "Portrait of a Nobleman"

Sala di Apollo
Among the most important paintings in the "Apollo Room" are "Mary Magdalene" and "Portrait of a Nobleman" (Titian), "Descent from the Cross" and "Holy Family" (Andrea del Sarto), "Cleopatra" (Guido Reni).

Sala di Marte
The most important paintings in the "Mars Room" include "Portrait of Luigi Cornaro" (Tintoretto), "The four Philosophers" (Rubens), "Madonna with the Rosary" (Murillo), "Consequences of War" (Rubens), "Cardinal Ippolito de' Medici" (Titian), "Cardinal Guido Bentivoglio" (Van Dyck).

Sala di Giove
The "Jupiter Room" is decorated with frescoes by Pietro da Cortona. Important works of art: "Three Ages of Man" (ascribed to Lorenzo Lotto, Giorgione and Bellini), "Madonna with the little Swallow" (Guercino), "John the Baptist" (Andrea del Sarto), "Descent from the Cross" (Fra Bartolommeo), "Donna Velata" i.e. Veiled Woman, or "La Fornarina", one of Raphael's finest portraits of women.

Sala di Saturno
In the "Saturn Room" the visitor should look out for "Madonna del Granduca", "Portrait of Tommaso Inghirami", "Portrait of Agnolo Doni", "Vision of Ezekiel", "Madonna with Baldachin", "Portrait of Magdalena Doni".

Palazzo Pitti

Sala di Apollo

Sala dell'Iliade
Of especial importance in the "Iliad Room" are "Portrait of Philip IV of Spain" (studio of Velázquez), "La Gravida" (Raphael), "Assumption of the Virgin" (two paintings on the same theme by Andrea del Sarto), "Count Waldemar Christian of Denmark" (Sustermans).

Other rooms
The tour continues through the Sala del Castagnoli ("Table of Apollo" or "Table of the Muses" by Dupré and Papi); the Sala delle Allegorie (with a fresco by Volterrano); the Sala delle Belle Arti (with 17th c. Florentine paintings); the Salone d'Ercole (with a painted ceiling by Benvenuti and a Sèvres vase); the Sala dell'Aurora (Vasari); the Sala di Berenice; Sala di Psiche (Salvatore Rosa); the Round Cabinet and Maria Luisa's bathroom; the Sala della Fama (French masters), the Sala dell'Arca; the Cappella delle Reliquie; the Sala della Musica (dei Tamburi); the Galleria del Poccetti (Rubens, Ribera); the Sala di Prometeo ("Madonna and Child", a masterpiece by Filippo Lippi, "Holy Family" by Signorelli, portrait of a man by Botticelli, "Apollo dancing with the Muses" by Peruzzi); the Corridoio delle Colonne (Flemish masters); the Sala di Flora ("Italian Venus", marble statue by Canova); the Sala dei Putti (Flemish masters, "The Three Graces" by Rubens); the Sala di Ulisse ("La Madonna dell'Impannata" by Raphael and "Death of Lucretia" by Filippino Lippi); the Saletta da Bagno; the Sala dell'Educazione di Giove (Caravaggio, Guercino); the beautiful Sala della Stufa ("The Four Ages of Man", wall-paintings by Pietro da Cortona).

Sala di Flora

Appartamenti ex Reali (Former Royal Apartments)

The collection of works of art in the Palazzo Pitti's Galleria Palatina is complemented by the Appartamenti ex Reali, the former Royal Apartments lived in by Victor Emmanuel II, Umberto I, Queen Margherita and Victor Emmanuel III. The magnificent rooms (the visitor should note the frescoes and stucco-work here, too) contain costly furniture, paintings, statues, tapestries and utensils.

Opening times
Tues.–Sat. 9 a.m.– 2 p.m.,
Sun. and public holidays
9 a.m.–1 p.m.

Closed
Mon.

Galleria d'Arte Moderna (Gallery of Modern Art)

The Gallery of Modern Art is on the second floor of the Pitti Palace. it was founded about 1860 and has been continuously expanded (by works of art transferred from other state or municipal galleries and by gifts). It gives an impressive general view of 19th and 20th c. painting in Tuscany and other parts of Italy. There are also excellent examples of 19th and 20th c. sculpture
A special section is devoted to the works of the "Macchiaioli" (the "daubers"). The representatives of this Tuscan school (including Giovanni Fattori, Silvestro Lega, Telemaco Signorini) owe their name to their anti-academic brushwork.
The final section is a collection of works by contemporary Italian painters, including Severini, Soffici, De Chirico and Morandi.

Opening times
Tues.–Sat. 9 a.m.– 2 p.m.,
Sun. and public holidays
9 a.m.–1 p.m.

Closed
Mon.

Palazzo Ricasoli

Museo degli Argenti (Silver Museum)

Opening times
Tues.–Sat. 9 a.m.–2 p.m.,
Sun. and public holidays
9 a.m.–1 p.m.

Closed
Mon.

The ground floor and mezzanine of the Palazzo Pitti house the silver collection, which in addition to the work of silversmiths and goldsmiths also has displays of precious stones, jewellery, carved ivory and amber, painted glass and porcelain.

The museum's collection, founded after the First World War, is based on the silver owned by the Medici family. Other exhibits come from the Uffizi (see Palazzo e Galleria Uffizi), the Bargello (Museo Nazionale del Bargello in the Palazzo del Bargello – see entry), and the treasures of the princely archbishops of Salzburg and the kings of Italy.

On display are 17th and 18th c. jewel caskets and reliquaries, 16th and 17th c. vases and crystalware, 16th and 17th c. tapestries, carved ivory and carved amber, the Medici's collection of jewellery, goblets, golden tableware, silver jugs and silver dishes.

Museo delle Carrozze (Coach Museum)

Opening times
Tues.–Sat. 9 a.m.–2 p.m.,
Sun. and public holidays
9 a.m.–1 p.m.

Closed
Mon.

Like the silver collection, the Coach Museum is also on the ground floor of the Pitti Palace.

On show are state coaches, barouches and carriages of every kind which were used by archdukes and kings in the 18th and 19th c., including the coaches of the Duke of Modena, Francesco II and King Ferdinando of Naples.

Palazzo Ricasoli H6

Location
Piazza Goldoni 2

Buses
A, 6, 9, 11, 36, 37

The house of the Ricasoli family stands in the Piazza Goldini, the square by the Ponte alla Carraia (see entry) over the Arno where seven streets converge. (The Ricasoli family also gave its name to a winery of repute in the Chianti district.) The building used to be ascribed to Michelozzo, but it was not begun until 1480 whereas Michelozzo lived from 1369 to 1472. It was completed in the early 16th c.

Palazzo Riccardi-Manelli (Formerly Palazzo Grifoni) K5

Location
Piazza della Santissima
Annunziata

Buses
B, 4, 6, 34

This imposing palace in Piazza della Santissima Annunziata (see entry) is the headquarters of the administrative authority of the province of Florence and of the Tuscany Regional Government. The three-storey building with its fine dignified façade opposite the church of Santissima Annunziata (see entry) dominates the square.

Ugolini Grifoni, a wealthy official under Grand Duke Cosimo I, commissioned the architect Bartolomeo Ammanati to erect a palace over the top of old houses, a task which he skilfully accomplished between 1557 and 1563. The combination of red brick and predominantly light-grey stone is especially effective.

*Palazzo Rucellai H6

Location
Via della Vigna Nuova 18

The architect Bernado Rossellino built this palace between 1446 and 1451 to designs by Leon Battista Alberti. It is one of Florence's finest Renaissance mansions. It was built for

Giovanni Rucellai, a wealthy merchant who acquired his money, refinement and standing in the 15th c.

Architect and artist, Alberti and Bernardo Rossellino, were given a free rein to show the full extent of their capabilities on the building; the prosperous merchant was only too pleased to provide the means. Their clarity of conception and breadth of execution can be seen in the finely-drawn façade with its tapering pilasters, variety of window shapes, carefully hewn blocks of ashlar and storeys of gradually diminishing height. Together they created a palace that was a milestone in the architectural history of the Renaissance. Above the windows of the first floor is a stone frieze of billowing sails, the trade-mark of the Rucellai family who still own the palace today.

The Loggia dei Rucellai (columned hall), built between 1460 and 1466 opposite the palace, is also worth seeing.

Next to the church of San Pancrazio (accessible from Via della Spada) is the Cappella Rucellai (see entries) with the Edicola del Santo Sepolcro.

Buses
A, 6, 11

Palazzo della Signoria

See Palazzo Vecchio

*Palazzo Spini-Ferroni   J6

The largest of Florence's medieval palaces, this was built in 1289, probably to plans by Arnolfo di Cambio. Restored in 1874, its massive walls, great height and emphatic crenellation make this extensive complex on the banks of the Arno most impressive. A medieval tower and a loggia on the ground floor have disappeared.

Location
Piazza Santa Trinità

Buses
A, B, 6, 11, 36, 37

**Palazzo Strozzi   J6

In the 15th c. the Strozzi family, who considered themselves just as good as the Medici, determined to outdo the ruler of Florence, Lorenzo de' Medici. Rather than erect a building that would vie with the Palazzo Medici-Riccardi (see entry) in terms of grandeur, the wealthy merchant Filippo Strozzi planned to build a house for his family that would be outstanding not for its size and splendour but for its meticulous workmanship. The Palazzo Strozzi was built between 1489 and 1538 and, in the year it was completed, it was seized by Cosimo I and withheld from the Strozzi family until 1568. Today it houses cultural institutes.

In this building the architects, Benedetto da Maiano and (after his death) Simone del Pollaiolo, known as Cronaca, achieved a combination of the greatest features of Renaissance architecture with articulation of classical beauty in the overall and detailed design and consummate craftsmanship in every aspect of the building. The impact of the façade depends on the balanced composition of the storeys, the portal, the windows and the cornice as well as on the art of the stonemason evident in every one of the ashlar blocks with horizontally-aligned bosses which project progressively less towards the top of the building.

Location
Piazza Strozzi

Buses
A, 6, 11, 36, 37

Palazzo dello Strozzino

The wrought-iron work (rings in the walls for tethering horses, torch-holders and lanterns on the corners) was executed around 1500 by Niccolò Grosso, a famous blacksmith, who accepted commissions only if paid in advance.

The elegant and graceful inner courtyard by Cronaca is worth visiting.

On the ground floor there is a small museum devoted to the history of the construction of the palace, including a wooden model of the palace by da Maiano.

The Galleria Strozzina (ground floor and first floor) has the Vicusseux Library and temporary exhibitions of art, both modern and from previous centuries.

Palazzo dello Strozzino   J6

Location
Piazza Strozzi 2

Buses
A, 6, 11

In 1458, before the Palazzo Strozzi (see entry) which now stands opposite had been built, the younger branch of the Strozzi family commissioned Michelozzo to build a house which was completed between 1462 and 1465 by Giuliano da Maiano.

In 1927 the area of the inner courtyard was incorporated into the Odeon Theatre, a project of the architect Marcello Piacentini.

Palazzo e Galleria degli Uffizi (Uffizi)   J6

Location
Piazza della Signoria/
Piazzale degli Uffizi
(entrance: Loggiato degli
Uffizi 6)

Buses
B, 13n, 19n, 23, 31, 32, 33

Opening times
Tues.–Sat. 9 a.m.–7.30 p.m.;
Sun. and public holidays
9 a.m.–1 p.m.

Closed
Mon.

Cosimo I de' Medici, Duke of Florence (and, after 1569, Grand Duke (Granduca) of Tuscany) moved out of the family palace (see Palazzo Medici) into the Palazzo Vecchio (see entry – also called Palazzo della Signoria) which therefore became the Palazzo Ducale (Ducal Palace). This left no room for the law-courts and governing body of Florence and plans were drawn up for offices of their own, the Uffizi, to be built adjoining the Palazzo Ducale. The foundation stone was laid in 1560. In 1565 a corridor was hastily built (in less than six months) from the Palazzo Vecchio through the Palazzo degli Uffizi and over the Ponte Vecchio to the Palazzo Pitti (see entries). The building (and the corridor) were designed and built by Vasari. Buontalenti continued to modify the Uffizi until 1586, but the loggias were glazed and made into a museum in 1581.

The Palazzo degli Uffizi encompassed the old customs building, the Zecca, where the famous coins, the "florins", were minted, and the Romanesque church of San Piero Scheraggio. This coincided with the construction of the studios and workshops where craftsmen worked with the semi-precious stones, the Pietre Dure, in which the Medici had always taken a passionate interest (see Opificio e Museo delle Pietre Dure). Rooms were also allocated for the study of the natural sciences and alchemy. In 1585–6 room was even found for a theatre where the first operas in the history of music were performed.

Today the palace houses the Uffizi Galleries and the National Archives.

The Palazzo degli Uffizi is U-shaped. One wing stretches from the Palazzo Vecchio (see entry) along one side of the Piazzale degli Uffizi to the Arno. A short section then runs alongside the

Galleria degli Uffizi

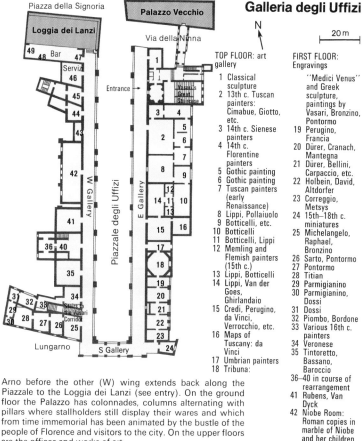

Piazza della Signoria

Palazzo Vecchio

Loggia dei Lanzi

Via della Ninna

N ↑

20 m

TOP FLOOR: art gallery

1 Classical sculpture
2 13th c. Tuscan painters: Cimabue, Giotto, etc.
3 14th c. Sienese painters
4 14th c. Florentine painters
5 Gothic painting
6 Gothic painting
7 Tuscan painters (early Renaissance)
8 Lippi, Pollaiuolo
9 Botticelli, etc.
10 Botticelli
11 Botticelli, Lippi
12 Memling and Flemish painters (15th c.)
13 Lippi, Botticelli
14 Lippi, Van der Goes, Ghirlandaio
15 Credi, Perugino, da Vinci, Verrocchio, etc.
16 Maps of Tuscany: da Vinci
17 Umbrian painters
18 Tribuna:

FIRST FLOOR: Engravings

"Medici Venus" and Greek sculpture, paintings by Vasari, Bronzino, Pontormo
19 Perugino, Francia
20 Dürer, Cranach, Mantegna
21 Dürer, Bellini, Carpaccio, etc.
22 Holbein, David, Altdorfer
23 Correggio, Metsys
24 15th–18th c. miniatures
25 Michelangelo, Raphael, Bronzino
26 Sarto, Pontormo
27 Pontormo
28 Titian
29 Parmigianino
30 Parmigianino, Dossi
31 Dossi
32 Piombo, Bordone
33 Various 16th c. painters
34 Veronese
35 Tintoretto, Bassano, Baroccio
36–40 in course of rearrangement
41 Rubens, Van Dyck
42 Niobe Room: Roman copies in marble of Niobe and her children (original lost)
43–50 in course of rearrangement

Arno before the other (W) wing extends back along the Piazzale to the Loggia dei Lanzi (see entry). On the ground floor the Palazzo has colonnades, columns alternating with pillars where stallholders still display their wares and which from time immemorial has been animated by the bustle of the people of Florence and visitors to the city. On the upper floors are the offices and works of art.

The uniform severely articulated façades conceal an irregular interior that developed from various 14th and 16th/17th c. buildings.

It was also the first building in Europe to use cement and iron struts.

Galleria degli Uffizi (Uffizi Gallery)

The art collection in the Uffizi was founded by the Medici, the one-time rulers of Florence and Grand Dukes of Tuscany. In the course of time it has developed into the most important art gallery in Italy and one of the best in the world with some 4000 paintings, including masterpieces by Italy's greatest 13th–18th c. artists and from other European countries. In addition

Location
Piazzale degli Uffizi/Piazza della Signoria

Buses
B, 13n, 19n, 23, 31, 32, 33

Palazzo e Galleria degli Uffizi

Opening times
Tues.–Sat. 9 a.m.–7.30 p.m.;
Sun. and public holidays
9 a.m.–1 p.m.

Closed
Mon.

there are dozens of priceless Classical sculptures as well as tapestries, drawings, jewellery, weapons, scientific instruments and archaeological finds – indicative of the unique and equally admirable patronage of the Medici

It is only very recently that it has been possible to compile a comprehensive catalogue of the host of objects, many of which are in storage.

(The 1966 flooding caused great damage in this gallery too.) To get to the actual collection of paintings from the Sala della Biglietteria (tickets) with frescoes by Andrea del Castagno and the "Annunciation" (1481), a masterpiece by Botticelli, the visitor can pass through the "Gabinetto dei Disegni e delle Stampe" (Engravings Room, drawings and prints; 104,000 items in storage alone); then come two vestibules with statues. After that the visitor reaches the galleries on the second floor extending right round the Piazzale degli Uffizi which are furnished with Roman marble statues and bronze figures, tapestries and rich wall-decoration.

The extent of the collection means that only the most outstanding works of art can be mentioned.

Room 2 (13th c. Tuscan school): "The Rucellai Madonna" by Duccio di Buoninsegna (*c.* 1285), "Madonna and Child and four Saints" and "Madonna with Angels and Saints" by Giotto (*c.* 1310), "Madonna in Maestà" by Cimabue (between 1280 and 1290).

Room 3 (14th c. Sienese school): "Annunciation with Saints" by Simone Martini (1333) and "Madonna in Glory" (1340) by Pietro Lorenzetti.

Room 4 (14th c. Florentine school): "St Matthew" by Andrea Orcagna and Jacopo di Cione (1367), "Pietà" (after Giotto) and "San Nicola da Bari" by Ambrogio Lorenzetti (1332).

Rooms 5 and 6 (Later Gothic schools): "Adoration of the Magi" by Lorenzo Monaco (1420), "Crucifixion" by Agnolo Gaddi, "Madonna and Child" by Jacopo Bellini, "Adoration of the Magi" by Gentile da Fabriano, his masterpiece, and "Coronation of the Virgin" by Lorenzo Monaco (1413).

Room 7 (early 15th c. Florentine school): one section of the famous "Battle of San Romano" by Paolo Uccello (1456), portraits by Piero della Francesca (1465), "Madonna and St Anne" by Masaccio and Masolino da Panicale (1420 or 1424), "Madonna in Majesty" by Domenico Veneziano and "Madonna and Child" and "Coronation of the Virgin" by Fra Angelico (1430 and 1435).

Room 8 (Room of the two Lippis, father and son): most of the paintings by Filippo and Filippino Lippi are scenes from the life of the Virgin.

Room 9 (Pollaiolo and Botticelli Room): "Portrait of an Unknown Man" (1470) and "Judith and Holofernes" by Botticelli (1487–92), and "Virtues" by Piero del Pollaiolo and Botticelli.

Titian: Venus of Urbino

Botticelli: Birth of Venus

Rooms 10–14: The main works in the room where the pictures have been rearranged (also possibly in other rooms) are "The Birth of Venus" (1486) and "La Primavera" ("Spring", 1477–8), two of Botticelli's masterpieces; other paintings by Botticelli are "Adoration of the Magi" (1475), "Pallas and the Centaur" (1485), "Madonna of the Magnificat" (1481–2), "Madonna with the Pomegranate" (1487) and "Calumny" (1494–5).

Other interesting paintings are those by Ghirlandaio, Filippino Lippi, Hans Memling (portrait), Roger van der Weyden ("Entombment") and the well-known "Portinari Triptych" by Hugo van der Goes.

Room 15 (15th c. Tuscan and Umbrian school): "Baptism of Christ" by Andrea Verrocchio (1470) and Leonardo da Vinci, works by Signorelli and Perugino, "Adoration of the Magi" by Leonardo da Vinci (1481), and "Annunciation", an early work by Leonardo da Vinci or Ghirlandaio (1470–5).

Room 17 (of the Hermaphrodite): Triptych and "Madonna delle Cave" by Andrea Mantegna, and Classical sculptures ("Hermaphrodite", "Cupid and Psyche").

Room 18 ("Tribuna"): In the centre is the "Medici Venus", the most renowned Classical marble sculpture in Florence (copy after Praxiteles); other important statues are the "Apollino" (after Praxiteles), "Arrotino" ("Scythian sharpening a Knife", 3rd or 2nd c. B.C. Pergamon school), "Wrestlers" (Pergamon school) and "Dancing Faun" (3rd c. B.C. copy).
The walls are mainly decorated with portraits of the Medici family (Vasari, Pontormo, Andrea del Sarto, Bronzino).

Room 19: Most of the paintings in this room are by Perugino (Don Biaggio Milanesi, the monk Baldassare, Francesco delle Opere and his 'Madonna between John and Sebastian") and by Luca Signorelli ("Holy Family" and "Madonna and Child").

Room 20 (German school): This room contains works by German masters. Lucas Cranach's "Martin Luther", "Katharina von Bora", "Self Portrait", "Saint George", another "Martin Luther", "Melanchthon" and "Adam and Eve". In the style of Cranach: "Portrait of a Lady", "John I", "Ferdinand III of Saxony"; "Portrait of a Young Man" by Joos van Cleve.
Albrecht Dürer's "Madonna and Child" ("Madonna with the Pear"), "Portrait of the Father" (1490), "Adoration of the Magi" (1504), an exemplary work, "Philip and James" and the drawing "Calvary".

Room 21 (15th and early 16th c. Venetians): "Holy Allegory" by Giovanni Bellini, and "Scenes from the Life of Moses".

Room 22 (16th c. German and Flemish painters): Works by Gerard David ("Adoration of the Magi"), Hans Holbein ("Portrait of Richard Southwell") and Albrecht Altdorfer ("St Florian").

Room 23 (Correggio Room): "Madonna", "Rest on the Flight into Egypt" and "Madonna in Glory" by Correggio; also two works ascribed to Raphael.

Botticelli:
"La Primavera"

Botticelli:
"Man with Medal"

P. della Francesca:
"Duchess Battista Sforza"

Rosso Fiorentini: "Cupid playing the Lute"

Room 24: 15th to 18th c. miniatures.

Rooms 25 and 26 (Michelangelo, Raphael and del Sarto Rooms): "The Holy Family" is the only (incomplete) panel definitely ascribed to Michelangelo. He created it between 1504 and 1505 for the wedding of Agnolo Doni and Magdalena Strozzi which is why it is also known as the Doni Tondo.

There are also works by Raphael (Portrait of Perugino), Fra Bartolommeo ("Vision of the Virgin") and Albertinelli. Masterpieces by Raphael are "Pope Leo X with Cardinals Giulio de' Medici and Luigi de' Rossi" (1518–19) and "The Madonna with the Goldfinch" (1506), also "Portrait of Francesco Maria della Rovere" and "Portrait of Julius II" (uncertain); also outstanding is Andrea del Sarto's "Madonna of the Harpies" (after the figures on the pedestal; 1517).

Room 27 (Pontormo Room): "Supper at Emmaus" and "Holy Family" by Pontormo (1525/1540).

Room 28 (Titian Room): Works by Titian in this room include his "Venus of Urbino" (1538), "Ludovico Beccadelli" (1552), "Venus and Cupid" (1560), "Eleonora Gonzaga della Rovere", "Francesco Maria, Duke of Urbino" and "Flora", one of his finest portraits of women.

Room 29: "Madonna with the Long Neck" and portrait of a man by Parmigianino.

Room 30: 16th c. Emilian schools.

Room 31 (Dosso Room): "La Fornarina" by Sebastiano del Piombo (1512) and "Head of a Youth" by Lorenzo Lotto (1505).

Room 32: Works by Sebastiano del Piombo, including "The Death of Adonis".

Passage 33 (Corridoio del Cinquecento): 16th c. Italian and foreign masters, including Clonet, Poppo, Zucchi, Amberger and Moro.

Room 34 (16th and 17th c. Venetians): "Holy Family with St Barbara", "Annunciation" and "Martyrdom of St Justina" by Veronese; portrait of a man by Tintoretto.

Room 35: "Leda", "Jacopo Sansovino", "Christ at the Well" and "The Samaritan Woman" by Tintoretto, Portrait of Francesco Maria della Rovere and "Madonna del Popolo" by Barocci.

Room 41: Portrait of Giovanni di Montfort by Antonis van Dyck. Some of Rubens' best works are here: "Henri IV at Ivry" and "Henri IV entering Paris", "Isabella Brandt" (his first wife) and "Entry of Ferdinand of Austria into Antwerp".

Rooms 42 to 50 are being rearranged so it is possible that works will not be found in the order given here.

Lucas Cranach: "Martin Luther"

Pontormo: "Cosimo the Elder"

Filippo Lippi: "Madonna and Child"

P. della Francesca: "Duke of Urbino"

Canaletto: Doges' Palace in Venice

Room 42 (Niobe Room): Pride of place in this room, built between 1779 and 1780, is taken by "Niobe and her Children", a Roman copy, discovered in Rome in 1583, of a 5th and 4th c. B.C. Greek original. It is the finest Classical sculpture in Florence after the Medici "Venus". In the middle is the "Medici Vase", a 2nd c. B.C. work; there are also Classical statues and paintings primarily by 18th c. artists (Canaletto).

Room 43: Flemish and Dutch painters.

Room 44: "Medusa", "Youthful Bacchus" (1589), "Sacrifice of Isaac" by Caravaggio (1590). Rembrandt's works in the Uffizi are "Self Portrait as an old Man" (1664), "Portrait of an old Man" (the so-called "Rabbi"; 1658 or 1666) and "Self Portrait as a young Man" (1633–4).

Between Room 35 and Room 34 is the entrance to Vasari's "corridor" (Corridoio Vasariano) which leads over the Arno by way of the Ponte Vecchio to the Palazzo Pitti (see entries). It houses self portraits by Italian and foreign painters.

The approximately 400 rooms of the National Archives in the Uffizi contain parchments and historical documents, currently undergoing reorganisation.

Palazzo Vecchio (Or Palazzo della Signoria) J/K6

The austere beauty of the city and the pride and tenacity of the people of Florence are embodied in the Palazzo Vecchio (or della Signoria) in a unique way. The city's principal palace came into existence when Florence was beginning its rise to power and greatness, was a witness to the decades of its artistic and cultural heyday and stayed on as the symbol of its glorious past. The defiant fortress-like structure of the main building serves to express the power exercised by the Florentine community from the 14th to the 16th c., while its bold and lofty tower symbolises the fierce pride of the people of Florence and the furnishings within the palace reflect their love of art.

Arnolfo di Cambio is said to have begun the building (1299–1314). Thereafter several patrons and architects (Michelozzo) were responsible for modifying the work and for the additions and alterations. At first the palace was the official residence of the Priors (Palazzo dei Priori) and of the Gonfaloniere, which made it the seat of the governing body of the Republic, the "Signoria".

Its other names, Palazzo del Popolo and Palazzo del Comune, are accounted for by the republican-democratic nature of Florence, even when it was ruled by the Medici, although they governed from their family palace, the Palazzo Medici (see entry). It was Cosimo I, Duke then Grand Duke of Tuscany, who moved into the city's principal palace in 1540, after which it was known as the Palazzo Ducale (Ducal Palace). Soon, however, he moved into the Palazzo Pitti, so the name of Palazzo Vecchio (old palace) became current. Between 1865 and 1872, during the Italian struggle for unity, it was for a while the seat of the Government, the Chamber of Deputies and the Foreign Ministry.

On the far left of the main entrance is a copy of Donatello's Marzocco, the heraldic lion of Florence with the city's coat of arms between its paws. Donatello's bronze statue of "Judith and Holofernes" (1455–60) has been moved inside the palace. On the right is a copy of Michaelangelo's "David" and a marble statue of Hercules and Cacus by Bandinelli (1533). Directly under the battlemented gallery are the coats of arms of the communes of Florence. The clock at the base of the tower dates from 1353.

The palace's exhibition rooms are on the ground, first and second floors.

The ground floor has three courtyards, the armoury and the great staircase leading to the upper floors. The first courtyard and the armoury are especially interesting.

Courtyard
The small inner courtyard, the "Primo Cortile", was redesigned by Michelozzo in 1470 (splendid columns!). In the centre is an elegant fountain with a putto and dolphin (1476), a copy of the original by Verrocchio which is now inside the palace. Around the top of the walls are 18 large townscapes, painted on the occasion of the wedding of Francesco de' Medici and Johanna of Austria (1565). Beneath the arcade is Perino da Vinci's marble group "Samson and the Philistine".

Location
Piazza della Signoria

Buses
B, 13n, 19n, 23, 31, 32, 33

Opening times
Mon.–Fri. 9 a.m.–7 p.m.;
Sun. and public holidays 8 a.m.–1 p.m.

Closed
Sat.

Exterior

Interior

Ground floor

Palazzo Vecchio

Armoury
The armoury is worth visiting as it is the only room to have survived from the 14th c. palace.

Staircase
The great staircase was the work of Vasari (1560–3).

First floor

Salone dei Cinquecento (Room of the Five Hundred)
This vast room (176 ft – 53·7 m long, 71·5 ft – 22·4 m high and 61·3 ft – 18·7 m wide) is the work of Simone del Pollaiolo, known as Cronaca (1495). The walls were once decorated with two famous paintings, Michelangelo's "Soldiers Bathing" and Leonardo's "Battle of Anghiari", but both have been lost. The ceiling is divided into 39 panels richly decorated with allegories and scenes from the history of Florence and of the Medici family.

On the left is what is known as the "Audience Room", which was reserved for receptions and official ceremonies, with niches containing statues of the Medici: Cosimo I, Pope Leo X, Giovanni delle Bande Nere, Allessandro, Pope Clement VII who was crowned by Emperor Charles V, Francesco I (by Bandinelli, de' Rossi and Caccini).

Against the opposite wall is Michelangelo's famous "Genius of Victory" ("Genio della Vittoria" – 1532–4), which was probably executed for the tomb of Pope Julius II in Rome. The statue shows the artist's supremely confident mastery in his shaping of the marble and his creative genius in the beauty and movement of the body. In the alcoves next to this are Roman statues: Ganymede, Mercury, Apollo and Bacchus.

Paintings, frescoes, statues ("Hercules" by Vincenzo de' Rossi) and tapestries complete the room's furnishings.

Quartiere di Leone X
Leo X's quarters lead off from the Salone dei Cinquecento (on the opposite side of the entrance, right). Today this is where the mayor and city council have their offices, which is why these rooms are not open to the public.

Studiolo di Francesco I de' Medici
To the right of the entrance a door leads to Francesco I's study, designed by Vasari and richly decorated with paintings, frescoes and statues. Eminent painters (Bronzino, Poppi, Tito, Naldini) and sculptors (Giambologna; 'Aeolus" or small Apollo) were employed on this "jewel casket" of Florentine late-Renaissance art.

Tesoretto
A secret staircase leads to the Tesoretto, Cosimo I's little study, with ceiling paintings by pupils of Vasari.

On the other side of the Salone dei Cinquecento (on a level with the "Audience Room") are the Ricetto (anteroom), the Sala degli Otto di Pratica and the Sala del Dugento with "Cosimo's bath".

Second floor

The following rooms may be visited on the second floor:

Sala dei Gigli (Lily Room)
The Lily Room has a large fresco by Ghirlandaio (1481–5).

Palazzo Vecchio
Palazzo
della Signoria

SECONDO PIANO

PRIMO PIANO

PIANTERRENO

SECOND FLOOR (SECONDO PIANO)
1 Sala degli Gigli
2 Guardaroba
3 Cancelleria, former office of N. Machiavelli
4 Sala dell'Udienza
5 Cappella della Signoria
6 Camera di Gualdrada
7 Camera di Penelope
8 Camera di Ester o Sala da Pranzo
9 Camera delle Sabine
10 Salotto
11 Camera verde
12 Cappella di Eleonora
13 Sala degli Elementi
14 Loggiato di Saturno
15 Camera di Ercole
16 Camera di Giove
17 Camera di Cibele
18 Camera di Cerere

FIRST FLOOR (PRIMO PIANO)
A Salone dei Cinquecento
B Udienza
1 "Il Genio della Vittoria", by Michelangelo
2 Studiolo di Francesco I de' Medici
3 Tesoretto, Cosimo I's writing desk, by Vasari
4 Sala dei Dugento
5 Sala degli Otto di Pratica
6 Ricetto
7 Sala del Duca Cosimo I
8 Sala di Lorenzo il Magnifico
9 Sala di Cosimo il Vecchio
10 Sala di Giovanni delle Bande Nere
11 Cappella di Leone X
12 Sala di Clemente VII
13 Sala di Leone X

GROUND FLOOR (PIANTERRENO)
A Primo Cortile (courtyard)
B Camera dell'Arme
C Scalone del Vasari

93

Cancelleria
In the Chancellery of the Secretary of the Republic stands a bust of Niccolò Machiavelli and the original of Verrocchio's "Putto and Dolphin" removed from the fountain in the courtyard.

Guardaroba
The cloakroom is fitted out with beautiful wooden presses.

Sala dell'Udienza
This Audience Room has a richly carved ceiling (by Giuliano da Maiano) and frescoes (including figures by Domenico Ghirlandaio).

Cappella della Signoria
This contains a large fresco by Ridolfo Ghirlandaio.

Quartiere di Eleonora di Toledo.
The apartments of the consort of Cosimo I, Eleonora of Toledo, who died at an early age in 1562, consist of the Camera di Gualdrada (the fresco on the bedroom ceiling shows the young Florentine woman who refused to kiss Emperor Otto IV because that was her husband's prerogative); Camera di Penelope (story of Odysseus); Camera di Ester or Dining Room (head of Apollo and fine lavabo); Salotto with interesting historical illustrations; Camera delle Sabine (ceiling painting: the Sabine women resolve the conflict between their menfolk and the Romans); Camera Verde, the "Green Room", with an adjoining study; Cappella di Eleonora (the paintings are by Bronzino).

Quartiere degli Elementi
The "Rooms of the Elements", decorated with paintings by Vasari and his pupil Gherardi (1556–66), consist of the Sala degli Elementi (allegories of Earth, Air, Fire and Water in the Mannerist style); Loggiato di Saturno (lovely view of Florence from the terrace); Camera di Ercole (scenes from the story of Hercules); Rooms of Juno, Jupiter, Cybele and Ceres and a small writing room.

"Ballatoio", tower room
From the "Ballatoio" it is possible to climb up to the tower room which affords a magnificent panoramic view of the city. The route to the top passes the Alberghettino, a prison cell, ironically christened the "little hotel", where Cosimo the Elder was incarcerated before he was sent into exile (1433) and where Savonarola was imprisoned (8–22 April 1498).

Quartiere del Mezzanino
The tour of the palace ends with a visit to the Quartiere del Mezzanino. The mezzanine, which Michelozzo created by lowering the ceilings, contains a display of works from the Collezione Loeser (paintings and sculptures by 14th and 16th c. Tuscan artists).

Palazzo Vecchio: Florence's principal palace ▶

Palazzo dei Vescovi (Bishops' Palace) L8

Location
On the Monte alle Croci

Bus
13

The palace, which was begun by Bishop Andrea dei Mozzi in 1295 near the church of San Miniato (see entry) and completed by his successor Antonio d'Orso in 1320, served the Bishops of Florence for a long time as their summer residence high above the city, until in 1534 it was made part of the monastery of S. Miniato. This building was subsequently also used as a military hospital, a Jesuit college and, on occasions, a concert hall.

The popes often spent long periods in Florence. Pope Stephen IX died here (buried in the church of Santa Reparata). His successor, Nicholas II, had previously been Bishop of Florence, an office which he retained.

Pazzi Chapel

See Santa Croce

Piazza di Bellosguardo

As the name suggests, there is a splendid view of Florence from the Piazza di Bellosguardo, SW of the centre, with the Villa di Bellosguardo and its beautiful garden. To the right of the Piazza stands the Villa Belvedere al Saracino (built by Baccio d'Agnolo in 1502 for Francesco Borgherini) and to the left is the Villa dell'Ombrellino. A bust of Galileo commemorates the fact that he lived here from 1617 to 1631.

Piazza del Duomo J/K5

Buses
1, 6, 7, 10, 11, 13r, 14, 17, 23, 25, 31, 32, 33

The Piazza del Duomo, the square around the cathedral (see Duomo Santa Maria del Fiore), is one of the most important sites in European art, with the cathedral, Giotto's Campanile and the Baptistery (see Battistero).

The cathedral square, adjoined on the W by the Piazza San Giovanni with the Archbishops' Palace (see Palazzo Arcivescovile), is overlooked by several imposing buildings, including the Loggia del Bigallo (see entry), the Palazzo della Misericordia, the Palazzo dei Canonici, the Palazzo Guadagni (see entry), the Museo dell'Opera del Duomo (see entry) and the Palazzo Niccolini.

Piazza de Santa Croce K6

Buses
13r, 14, 19n, 23, 31, 32, 33

In front of the church of Santa Croce (see entry) is a square which would have been considered unusually large in the Middle Ages. It was obviously intended for festivals and popular assembly or as a site for the Franciscan monks to preach their sermons. A type of football was played here as early as the 16th c.; a commemorative plaque on the façade of the Palazzo dell'Antella marks a boundary line.

Focal points are the 17th c. fountain on the W side of the square, the large monument to Dante and two Palazzi.

* Piazza di Santa Maria Novella   H5

In the bustling five-sided Piazza in front of the church of Santa Maria Novella near the Loggia di San Paolo (see entries) stand two marble obelisks surmounted by bronze lilies and supported by four tortoises (By Giambologna; 1608). They mark the ends of the course of the annual chariot race, the "Palio dei Cocchi".

Buses
9, 13, 14, 17, 19, 22, 23, 36, 37

* Piazza della Santissima Annunziata   K5

Judged the most beautiful square in Florence, the tone of the spacious Piazza della SS. Annunziata is set by four buildings of artistic importance – the church of Santissima Annunziata (see entry) at the top, the portico by Brunelleschi of the foundling hospital, the Spedale degli Innocenti (see entry) on the right, the colonnades of the Confraternità dei Servi di Maria, the work of Antonio da Sangallo and Baccio d'Agnolo, on the left and Ammanati's Palazzo Grifoni (see entry).
In the middle of the square are the equestrian statue of Grand Duke Ferdinand I (Giambologna's last work, completed by his pupil Tacca in 1608) and two fountains with sea-creatures in bronze, the work (1629) of Pietro Tacca from Carrara, sculptor, caster of metals and architect rolled into one, and his assistants.

Buses
B, 1, 4, 6, 7, 10, 11, 17, 25, 34

* Piazza della Signoria con Fonte di Piazza (Neptune Fountain)   J6

The Piazza della Signoria has been the political centre of the city since the 14th c. when houses belonging to Ghibelline families had to make way for the new square. The square is notable for its important buildings and statues – the Palazzo Vecchio, Palazzo degli Uffizi, Loggia dei Lanzi (see entries) and the statues by Michelangelo and Donatello (some of the originals are in the Galleria dell'Accademia, see entry).
There are also two memorials here: a small disc in the pavement, not far from the Neptune Fountain, marks the place where Savonarola and his companions Buonvicini and Maruffi were hanged and burned at the behest of Pope Alexander VI.
Near the fountain stands the equestrian statue of Cosimo I who had been elevated to the title of Grand Duke of Tuscany by Pope Leo V in 1569. The statue, by Giambologna, dates from 1594.
The most impressive monument in the square, however, is the Fonte di Piazza (del Nettuno), the Fountain of Neptune.
The Piazza della Signoria was to be decorated with a magnificent work of art for the wedding of Francesco de' Medici, son of Cosimo I, to Princess Johanna of Austria (1565), since through this marriage the Medici were rising into the ranks of the great ruling houses of Europe and Francesco even received the title of Grand Duke. Consequently a fountain which had already been begun to the left of the entrance to the Palazzo Vecchio had to be swiftly completed. Between 1563 and 1575 Bartolommeo Ammanati and his assistants made it the largest fountain in Florence, with the god Neptune, four horses and three tritons.
The work possibly proceeded with too much haste, for the people of Florence jeered: "Ammanato, Ammanato, che bel marmo hai rovinato." ("What fine marble you have ruined!")

Buses
B, 19n, 23, 31, 32

*Piazzale Michelangelo   L7

Bus
13

Florence's finest viewpoint is named after the artist who did not always receive the best of treatment from the people of Florence. It was designed by Giuseppe Poggi and laid out between 1865 and 1870. In hardly any other city in the world can well-known landmarks be as easily identified with the aid of a map as they can be here.

In the middle of the square are statues commemorating Michelangelo: bronze copies of "David" and of his four statues ("Times of the Day") for the Medici tombs in San Lorenzo (see entry).

Pinacoteca dello Spedale degli Innocenti

See Spedale degli Innocenti

Poggio a Caiano

Location
18 km (12 miles) NW
(55, 66)

About 18 km (12 miles) NW of Florence, in the village of Poggio a Caiano, stands the Villa Medicea, generally considered to be the Medici's finest and most splendid summer residence. It was built by Giuliano da Sangallo for Lorenzo the Magnificent. The Medici loved this residence and had alterations and extensions carried out in later years.

Yet again details such as the entrance loggia, the terracotta reliefs in the entrance hall, the large drawing room with its frescoes by Andrea del Sarto, Pontormo, Franciabigio and Allori ("Cicero's return from Exile", "Caesar accepting Tribute from Egypt", "Vertunno and Pomona") testify to the artistic sensibilities of the Medici.

King Victor Emmanuel II, who lived here with his morganatic wife, the Contessa di Mirafiori, also left it fine furniture and decorations.

The villa has a lovely garden as well.

Ponte alla Carraia (Bridge)   H6

Buses
A, 6, 9, 11, 36, 37

The second oldest bridge over the Arno collapsed several times and had to be rebuilt, as for example in 1304 when the bridge was crowded with spectators trying to watch a spectacle on the Arno, or as a result of flooding. It was built in its present form, with five arches, by Ammanati in 1559.

The Ponte alla Carraia was also blown up by German troops during the Second World War but it was possible to rebuild the bridge in its original form.

Ponte alle Grazie (Bridge)   K6/7

Buses
B, 13, 19, 23, 31, 32, 33

The first bridge upstream of the Ponte Vecchio (see entry) is the Ponte alle Grazie which was built in 1237 on the orders of Mandella, Podestà of Florence. The bridge withstood the 1333 flood but was so badly damaged in the Second World War that it had to be rebuilt in its modern form. The name of the bridge comes from a nearby chapel dedicated to the Virgin.

Piazzale Michelangelo: bronze copy of Michelangelo's "David" ▶

Ponte Santa Trinità (Bridge) H/J6

Buses
A, B, 6, 11, 36, 37

The Ponte Santa Trinità is the most elegant bridge in Florence. It was first built in 1252 but soon collapsed. Rebuilt more solidly in stone, it was again destroyed when the Arno burst its banks in 1333 and 1557. It was built in its present form by Ammanati between 1567 and 1570 (reportedly in consultation on artistic matters with Michelangelo).

When it was blown up by German troops in 1944 the people of Florence gathered up the fragments which made it possible to rebuild it in its original form between 1955 and 1957.

On the corners of the bridge stand allegorical figures of the four seasons; they were placed here in 1608.

** Ponte Vecchio (Old Bridge) J6

Bus
B

It is possible that the Ponte Vecchio, the "Old Bridge", at the narrowest point on the river dates back to Etruscan times. It is known for certain this is where there was a wooden bridge for the Roman consular road, the Via Cassia, to cross the Arno. On account of its age the Ponte Vecchio has had to undergo more repair following collapse or flooding than any other bridge in the city.

Shops and dwellings have been built on it since the 13th c. It was handy for the butchers who could throw their waste straight into the river, to the delight of the fish and those Florentines who had to keep the city clean. The number of

Ponte Vecchio: the "Old Bridge" at the Arno's narrowest point

shops increased to such an extent, however, that Grand Duke Ferdinando I decreed "for the benefit of strangers" that only goldsmiths might have shops on the bridge, a ruling that has been observed right up to the present.

In the middle of the bridge is a bust of the famous Florentine goldsmith Benvenuto Celini (1900). At first-floor level above the shops is the Corridoio Vasariano, the passage linking the Palazzo Vecchio to the Palazzo Pitti (see entries). When it was built in the 16th c. the corridor had to be taken round the Mannelli tower on brackets since the Mannelli family refused to allow it to be built through their tower.

Porta alla Croce

M6

Of the city's defensive walls only the Porta alla Croce, the Cross Gate, in Piazza Beccaria, built in 1284, remains. Inside is a seriously damaged fresco by Michele di Ridolfo, "Madonna and Child with St John the Baptist and St Ambrose".

Location
Piazza Beccaria

Porta Romana (City Gate)

G7

The Via Cassia, the road that led to and from Rome, passes through the Porta Romana, the Roman Gate, largest and best-preserved of Florence's city gates. Above the arch inside the gatehouse, which was built in 1326, is a fresco of the 14th c. Florentine school, "Madonna and Child and Four Saints" (Franciabigio).

Location
Via Romana

Buses
B, 38, 42

Porta alla Croce

Porta Romana

Porta San Frediano (Or Porta Pisana; City Gate)   G6

Location
Borgo S. Frediano

Buses
A, 6

From the Arno a section of the old city wall leads to the Porta San Frediano. This gate is also known as Porta Pisana because it was from here that the road to Pisa left the city. This massive structure was built between 1332 and 1334, probably to designs by Andrea Pisano. The formidable doors are 43.3 ft (13.2 m) high and 10 in. (25 cm) thick.

Porta San Giorgio (City Gate)   J7

Location
Costa S. Giorgio

The Porta San Giorgio, completed in 1260, is part of the second circle of walls on the left bank of the Arno, the course of which can still be traced from the positions of the city gates of San Niccolò (see entry), San Miniato, San Giorgio and Porta Romana and San Frediano (see entries).
The interior fresco of the Madonna is by Bicci di Lorenzo; on the outside is a relief of St George.

Porta San Niccolò (City Gate)   L7

Location
Piazza Poggi

Buses
8, 13n, 23r

The Porta San Niccolò was equally suited for defence by land and, in conjunction with the Zecca tower on the opposite bank of the Arno, for sealing off the river. The tower of the bastion, built in 1324, forms the beginning of the city wall in the E on the left bank of the Arno.

Rotonda del Brunelleschi   K5
(Officially: Rotonda di Santa Maria degli Agnoli or Angeli)

Location
Via degli Alfani

Buses
B, 6, 34

The Rotonda di Santa Maria degli Agnoli (or Angeli), also known as Rotonda del Brunelleschi, forms the nucleus of an octagonal church which Brunelleschi began after 1433 for the cloth-merchants' guild but never completed. The Rotonda is thought to be the first Renaissance building to be based on a central plan. In 1936 neighbouring buildings were demolished with the result that the Rotonda is now free-standing.

Rucellai Chapel

See San Pancrazio

San Carlo dei Lombardi (San Carlo Borromeo; Church)   J6

Location
Via Calzaiuoli

Buses
B, 6, 7, 11, 19n, 23, 31, 32, 33

Opposite Orsanmichele (see entry) is the little Gothic single-naved church of San Carlo which was built between 1349 and 1404 first by Neri di Fioravante and Benci di Cione and then by Simone Talenti. It did not get its present name until the 17th c. when it was entrusted to the care of Lombards. St Carlo Borromeo was a bishop of Milan. Until then it had been dedicated to St Michael and St Anne.

San Felice (Church)   H7

The history of the church, which stands opposite the Palazzo Pitti (see entry), extends far back into the Middle Ages (1066). The façade, a classic example of simple yet effective Renaissance architecture, was built about 1450. The church contains works by the Giotto school ("Christ Crucified"), by the schools fo Filippino Lippi (triptych), Ridolfo Ghirlandaio ("Madonna and Child"), and of Neri di Bicci (triptych) and a terracotta group from the school of Giovanni della Robbia.

Location
Piazza San Felice

Bus
B

*San Firenze (Church)   K6

The Baroque complex of San Firenze is in the Piazza San Firenze not far from the city's main square, the Piazza della Signoria (see entry). It was built when members of the brotherhood of priests of St Philip Neri came to Florence (c. 1640).
On the square there are two church façades with a palace between them. The church of San Filippo Neri was built by Gherardo Silvani (1633–48) on the site of an old oratory dedicated to San Fiorenzo (hence the derivation of the name Firenze).
The former church of Sant'Appolinare, together with the palace, is today the seat of the Tribunale, the judicial authority. When Florence was the country's capital before the unification of Italy the buildings were also used as the Ministry of the Interior.
These court buildings contain one of the most impressive Baroque staircases in Florence. The façades of the two churches, added to the porches in 1715, were designed by Ferdinando Ruggieri.

Location
Piazza San Firenze

Buses
13n, 19n, 23, 31, 32, 33

San Frediano in Cestello (Church)   H6

This Carmelite church and convent were formerly known as Santa Maria degli Angeli and then became a parish church dedicated to St Frediano. The church was transformed in the 17th c. when it assumed a Baroque character, as is evidenced by its distinctive little cupola and graceful campanile.
Inside is the famous "Smiling Madonna", a 13th/14th c. Tuscan painted wooden statue.

Location
Piazza di Cestello

San Gaetano (Church)   J5

The finest 17th c. façade in Florence belongs to the Baroque church of San Gaetano. The original 11th c. church (San Michele Berteldi) was completely rebuilt in the early 17th c. Inside, pale figures against black stone imbue the place with a special atmosphere. In the second chapel on the left is "The Martyrdom of St Laurence" by Pietro da Cortona.
In the Cappella Antinori in the adjoining monastery is a "Christ Crucified" by Filippo Lippi.

Location
Piazza Antinori

Buses
A, 22

103

San Giovanni(no) dei Cavalieri (Church) K4

Location
Via San Gallo 66/70

Buses
B, 1, 20, 25, 34

The name of the church of San Giovanni(no) dei Cavalieri (of the Maltese Knights of St John) changed as often as did the architects. First it was "Oratory of Mary Magdalene" as a home for "fallen" girls (1326), then "San Pier Celestino" "San Niccolò" (1533), and finally "San Giovanni Decollato" (The Beheaded John The Baptist) or "San Giovanni dei Cavalieri", the patron saint of nuns from Jerusalem who had a convent (with a fine cloister) near the church.
Inside is a "Nativity" (1435) by di Lorenzo and a "Coronation of the Virgin" by di Bicci.

* San Giovanni degli Scolopi (Church) J5

Location
Via Martelli/Via de' Gori

Buses
B, 1, 4, 6, 7, 10, 11, 13r, 19r, 23, 25, 31, 32, 33

Next to the patron saint of Florence, John the Baptist, stands John the Evangelist. It was in his honour that the architect Ammanati began to build this church and the adjacent college for the Jesuits opposite the Palazzo Medici (see entry).
The Jesuits were followed by the Scolopi priests. After Ammanati's death (1592) the architect Alfonso Parigi the Younger completed the building work (1661). The façade and the interior, which is richly adorned with frescoes and marble, show that on this church no expense was spared.

San Jacopo sopr'Arno (Church) J6

Location
Borgo San Jacopo 34

Buses
B, 11, 36, 37

From the Ponte Trinità (see entry) there is a splendid view of the little Romanesque church of San Jacopo "on the Arno" (12th c.) with its beautiful Campanile (1660). The church has a porch dating from about 1000, the only one of this period in Florence. Inside are frescoes and altarpieces painted by 18th c. Florentine artists.
Near the church, on the corner of Borgo San Jacopo and Via dello Sprone, is a lovely fountain by Buontalenti.

** San Lorenzo, Cappelle Medicee, J5
Biblioteca Mediceo-Laurenziana
(Church with Medici Chapel and Laurenziana Library)

Location
Piazza San Lorenzo

Buses
1, 4, 6, 7, 10, 11, 13, 14, 17, 23, 25, 31, 32, 33

San Lorenzo ranks as one of the most important art sites in the Western world. The church of St Laurence, the "Old Sacristy", the "New Sacristy", the "Princes' Chapel" and the "Lauren-ziana Library" are works of the highest architectural importance in their own right and house priceless art treasures. It was here, in their parish church, that the Medici, unrivalled as patrons, spurred on the artists of their city – Brunelleschi, Donatello and Michelangelo – to ever greater achievements.
It is said that the church of San Lorenzo was founded by St Ambrose in 393 outside the city walls of that time. It was rebuilt in the 11th c. in the Romanesque style. It was that important exponent of Florentine Renaissance architecture, Brunelleschi, who was commissioned by the Medici (from 1419 onwards) to

give it its present form. The work was completed after his death but in accordance with his plans by Antonio Manetti (1447–60). Michelangelo supplied designs (drawings and models in the Casa Buonarroti – see entry) for the façade but they were never implemented, so the bare bricks are still visible. To the right of the façade in the Piazza San Lorenzo is the monument to Giovanni delle Bande Nere (1360–1429), father of Cosimo I and founder of the ducal Medici dynasty (by Baccio Bandinelli, 1540).

Brunelleschi's light, harmonious interior of the church displays the clear-cut articulation of the Renaissance architecture: a beautiful marble pavement, columns with Corinthian capitals supporting the broad arches, an intricate coffered ceiling with delicate rosettes. The harmonious proportions of the church's side chapels, aisles and nave denote architecture of the highest order.

Interior of the church

It is richly furnished throughout with important works of art, of which the following sections list the most outstanding.

Nave
At the end of the nave are two bronze pulpits by Donatello, the artist's final masterpiece (*c.* 1460), completed by his pupils Bartolomeo Bellano and Bertoldo di Giovanni, vividly depicting scenes from the life of Christ and the saints.

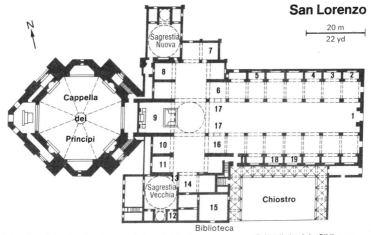

San Lorenzo

20 m
22 yd

1 Façade wall, by Michelangelo
2 "Martirio di San Sebastiano", by Empoli
3 "Sposalizio di Maria", by R. Fiorentino (1523)
4 "San Lorenzo", by N. Lapi
5 "Adorazione dei Magi", by G. Macchietti
6 Marble tabernacle, by D. da Settignano
7 Tomb of Maria Anna Carolina
8 Monument to Pietro Benvenuti

9 Cappella Maggiore
10 Wooden statue, "Madonna col Bambino" (late 14th c.)
11 Altar, by the school of Ghirlandaio
12 Marble basin, by the school of Donatello
13 Tomb of Pietro and Giovanni de' Medici, by A. del Verrocchio (1472)
14 Cappella di Ss Cosma e Damiano

15 Vestibule of the Biblioteca Mediceo-Laurenziana
16 "Martirio di San Lorenzo", by Bronzino (1565–9)
17 Bronze pulpits, by Donatello and his pupils
18 "Martirio di Sant'Arcadio e Compagni", by Sogliani
19 "Crocifisso tra la Madonna e San Giovanni" (15th and 17th c.)

Left aisle

Above the door to the cloister is a marble balcony thought to have been designed by Donatello.

Opposite Donatello's bronze pulpit is a fresco by Agnolo Bronzino, "Martyrdom of St Laurence" (1569).

Left arm of transept

In the Cappella Martelli (left) are a diptych by Filippo Lippi, "Annunciation" (1440; on the altar), one of his major works, and a monument to Donatello (1896) by Dario Guidotti and Raffaello Romanelli.

Cloister

From the left aisle a door leads to the cloister of San Lorenzo built in the style of Brunelleschi (1475). From here there is a magnificent view of the Campanile and the dome of Florence Cathedral (see Duomo).

Old Sacristy

The left arm of the transept leads into the Sagrestia Vecchia (old sacristy). Intended by its founder, Giovanni Bicci de' Medici, to be a burial chapel but linked with the public function of a sacristy, it was Brunelleschi's first complete architectural work (1420–8), and in its construction, articulation and proportions was to have a profound influence on European architecture.

Here, too, the impact of the building is heightened by works of art. Four medallions under the dome show scenes from the life of St John the Evangelist and four stucco reliefs in the arches depict the four Evangelists. These are all by Donatello as are the bronze doors in the apse representing martyrs and apostles in animated discourse.

On the left-hand wall is the magnificent tomb of Piero and Giovanni de' Medici (sons of Cosimo the Elder) by Andrea Verrocchio (1472). Under the marble table in the middle is the sarcophagus of Giovanni Bicci de' Medici and his wife Piccarda Bueri (the parents of Cosimo the Elder).

Cappella Maggiore (Great Chapel)

On the high altar is a "Crucifixion" by Baccio da Montelupe.

Right aisle

Opposite Donatello's bronze pulpit (in the side chapel) is a tabernacle by Desiderio da Settignano (1461).

In the last chapel but one (going towards the exit) is a painting by Rosso Fiorentino, "The Marriage of the Virgin" (1523).

*Biblioteca Mediceo-Laurenziana (Laurentian Library)

Opening times
Tues.–Sat. 10 a.m.–1 p.m.

Closed
Mon., Sun., public holidays

The Biblioteca Laurenziana, built on to the church of San Lorenzo and its cloister, owes its artistic importance, its architecture and its contents to the Medici family. The library was founded by Cosimo the Elder as a collection of documents and books and enlarged by Lorenzo the Magnificent. It was transferred to Rome but part of is was returned to Florence under Pope Clement VII (also a Medici), who gave the orders for a building in which the public could have access to the collection. Building commenced in 1524 to designs by Michelangelo.

Biblioteca Mediceo-Laurenziana: designed by Michelangelo

Despite the difficult external conditions – it had to be built on the weak foundations of a 13th c. monastery – the library was consecrated in 1571. It shows that Michelangelo, who, after he left Florence in 1534, continued to take part in the building work by means of letters and models, was at the height of his powers as an architect. The importance of the Biblioteca Laurenziana as a work of art is due to the three-dimensional articulation of the façade, the vestibule and the reading room, the staircases, and the confident use of all the decorative elements of Renaissance architecture.

The collection of manuscripts includes important papers from Ancient Egypt and valuable manuscripts by Napoleon.

**Cappelle Medicee (Medici Chapels with the tombs of the Medici)

Although the Medici Chapels form part of San Lorenzo they are now run as a museum in their own right, separately from the church. They consist of the Medici family vault (Cappella dei Medici) and the New Sacristy (for the oldest Medici Chapel, see San Lorenzo, Old Sacristy).

Location
San Lorenzo, Piazza
Madonna degli Aldobrandini

Opening times
Tues.–Sat. 9 a.m.–7 p.m.;
Sun. and public holidays
9 a.m.–1 p.m.

Closed
Mon.

Crypt
From the crypt, with tombs of members of the Medici family, the visitor ascends to the Cappella dei Principi, the Chapel of the Princes, mausoleum of the Medici grand dukes.

In 1602 Grand Duke Ferdinando I had the idea of building a particularly splendid family vault for the Medici dynasty. The plans were so sumptuous that the rumour went round that the

Cappella dei Medici

intention was to transfer the tomb of Jesus Christ from Jerusalem to Florence, for such an extravagant building could not be intended for mortal men, not even for princes.

The final design came from Giovanni de' Medici (illegitimate son of Cosimo I) and was put into effect by the architect Buontalenti (1604 onwards). After his death the work was continued by Mario Nigetti (until 1640). Despite a great deal of effort the chapel was not completed until the death in 1737 of the last Medici to rule Florence; the huge dome, 194 ft (59m) high but very heavy-looking, was not completed until the 19th c. The furnishings attest to the importance of the Medici family: ceiling paintings showing scenes from the Old and New Testaments, precious mosaics on the walls, 16 coats of arms of Tuscan cities inlaid with semi-precious stones and, high above, the huge coat of arms of the Medici.

Six Medici Grand Dukes are buried in the Chapel: they are (clockwise) Cosimo I (d. 1574), Francesco I (d. 1587), Cosimo III (d. 1723), Ferdinando I (d. 1609), Cosimo II (d. 1621) and Ferdinando II (d. 1670). Their wall tombs and sarcophagi, executed with artistry and costly materials, were the work of highly skilled craftsmen, but the gloomy pomp of the chapel has a chilling air about it, an indication that the heyday of Renaissance art came and went with the 16th c. Behind the altar is the entrance to the reliquary and treasure chapels.

New Sacristy
(Sagrestia Nuova)

The Cappella dei Principi leads into the Sagrestia Nuova, the New Sacristy (as distinct from Brunelleschi's Old Sacristy in the church), where Michelangelo's art reached the peak of perfection.

Cardinal Giulio de' Medici and Pope Leo X (also a Medici) commissioned Michelangelo to build their family a funerary chapel near the church of San Lorenzo. This chapel was the artist's first work as an architect and to which he also applied his twin talents as a painter and a sculptor. This can be seen in the articulation of the internal walls, the three-dimensional treatment given to the architectural elements, the niches and pediments, arches and gables, both projecting and inset. The interior with its predominant "colours" of dark grey and brilliant white was evenly lit by the windows in the dome.

As well as his commission as architect Michelangelo was also called upon to sculpt the tombs for members of the Medici family. He completed only two of the tombs, however, those of Giuliano, Duke of Nemours, and Lorenzo, Duke of Urbino. (Lorenzo the Magnificent, his brother Giuliano, who was murdered in 1478, and Duke Alessandro, who was murdered in 1537, are also buried in the chapel but have no monuments.) Neither Giuliano, as generalissimo of the Church of Rome with the military commander's baton, nor Lorenzo with the grotesque helmet on his head (maybe a sign of his feeble-mindedness) are depicted as definite personalities, nor did the artist intend them to be. There is no satisfactory explanation either as to why the statues of "Night" (with the crescent moon and stars in her hair, and accompanied by a poppy, an owl and a mask) and "Day" (unfinished) were assigned to Giuliano, while on his tomb Lorenzo has the statues of "Dawn" and "Dusk". It is not known whether their designation is as Michelangelo intended or whether as themes they are even

Cappelle Medicee: exterior ▶

Cappelle Medicee: interior of the New Sacristy

appropriate. What is more likely is that the artist used the exquisitely carved marble figures to express the contrasts between Life and Death, sleeping and waking, man and woman, to symbolize the Active and the Contemplative life with six statues that in the art of sculpture are unsurpassed. Michelangelo worked on both tombs between 1524 and 1533. During the same period he also worked on the intensely emotional "Madonna and Child" (on the sarcophagus of Lorenzo the Magnificent and his brother Giuliano) but did not manage to complete it.

*San Marco e Museo di San Marco   K4/5
(Church and Museum of San Marco)

Location
Piazza San Marco

Buses
B, 1, 4, 6, 7, 10, 11, 17, 20, 25, 34

The church of San Marco, built in 1299 by the Silvestrine order of monks, together with the monastery was transferred to the Dominicans of Fiesole (see entry) by Pope Eugene IV in the year of the Cathedral's consecration (1436). Thanks to the generosity of Cosimo the Elder the church was largely reconstructed and the monastery was completely rebuilt. The work was entrusted to the architect Michelozzo (1431–52). Giambologna added the side altars, the Chapel of St Antonino and the Salviati Chapel in 1588. The church underwent alterations by Pier Francesco Silvani in 1678 and the façade was reworked in 1780.

Interior

The single-naved church contains valuable paintings and furnishings. The following are of interest (clockwise).

San Marco: exterior (left) and cloister of St Antonino (right)

Interior of the façade
In the centre is an interesting "Crucifixion" in the style of Giotto.

The Salviati Chapel (built in 1588 by Giambologna) and the Serragli Chapel are at the far end. Both contain notable paintings and sculptures.

Right
Returning to the exit along the right-hand side, the visitor will notice:
A Baroque marble door designed by Cigoli that leads to the sacristy.
A Byzantine mosaic, "Virgin in Prayer" (705–707) from the Oratory of Pope John VII in Rome.
A painting, "Madonna and Child" by Fra Bartolommeo della Porta.
The oldest part of the monastery surrounding the church houses the museum, while monks still live in the rest of the monastery buildings.

Museo di San Marco

The monastery of San Marco, built in Renaissance style by Michelozzo, with its superb collection of paintings and frescoes, gives a better idea than the church of the spiritual life of the Dominicans and their interest in art.
In the late 15th and early 16th c. San Marco was the source of strong religious impulses that temporarily transformed Florence. Besides the Dominican monk Antoninus, later to

Opening times
Tues.–Sat. 9 a.m.–2 p.m.;
Sun. and public holidays
9 a.m.–1 p.m.

Closed
Mon.

111

become Archbishop of Florence and St Antonino, there was Savonarola, the revivalist preacher who was Prior of San Marco until he was hanged and burned in 1498.

The monastery owes its fame, however, to the Dominican monk Fra Angelico who painted the rooms of the convent between 1436 and 1445, thus leaving us today with a "natural" museum. Fra Bartolommeo, an inspired early 16th c artist, is also represented here by a number of his paintings.

The following are the works of major importance.

Ground floor

Pilgrims' hospice
Here there are panels by the Blessed Angelico from various museums in Florence, including "Madonna dei Linaioli" (1436, commissioned from Angelico by the linen weavers' guild), miniatures of the life of Jesus (1450), the famous "Deposition" (1435) and the "Last Judgement" (1430).

Cloister of St Antonino
Immediately opposite the entrance is the fresco, "St Dominic at the Foot of the Cross"; diagonally opposite the entrance, in the lunette, is the fresco, "Ecce Homo" (both by Fra Angelico).

Great Refectory
The paintings worth seeing in the Great Refectory include Fra Bartolommeo's fresco of the "Last Judgement".

Sala del Lavabo
Here there is another impressive work by Fra Bartolommeo, his large panel, "Madonna with St Anne and other Saints" (1510).

Chapter House
The whole of one wall of the chapter house, where the monks confessed and atoned for their sins, is taken up by Fra Angelico's fresco of the "Crucifixion".

Small Refectory
In the Small Refectory is a famous "Last Supper" by Ghirlandaio, similar to the one in the Ognissanti church (see entry).

First floor

On the first floor are over 40 cells which Fra Angelico and his assistants adorned with frescoes. His style is unmistakable in all the paintings and frescoes. He transforms the severity, stiffness and rigidity of the medieval saints into delicateness, softness and charm. His saints are innocent and pious yet their features are not ethereal but entirely human. Man appears transfigured, the earthly bears traces of the celestial. There is scarcely a more intimate representation of the "Annunciation" than the one by Fra Angelico (third room on the left after the stairs).

At the far end are the rooms occupied by Savonarola as Prior, containing mementoes and his portrait by Fra Bartolommeo, and the cell of St Antonino, Archbishop of Florence. The last two cells on the side overlooking the church recall the memory of Cosimo the Elder who often came here in retreat when he was ruler of the city.

Library: The great hall of the library, the work of Michelozzo (1444), is notable for the austere beauty of its architecture and contains valuable manuscripts, missals and bibles.

Fresco by Fra Angelico: "La Madonna della Stella" ▶

San Michelino – San Michele Visdomini (Church) K5

Location
Via de' Servi

Buses
1, 6, 7, 10, 11, 13r, 14, 17, 19r, 23, 25, 31, 32, 33

In the shadow of the cathedral (see Duomo Santa Maria del Fiore) is the church of San Michelino, the Vicedomini family church (hence the name San Michele Visdomini), that had to make way for the cathedral and was rebuilt a few yards away in the 14th c. (renovated in the 17th c.).
It contains altarpieces by Pontormo ("Holy Family and Saints"), Passignano, Empoli and Poppi.

**San Miniato al Monte (Church) L8

Location
Monte alle Croci

Bus
13

A visit to the church of San Miniato al Monte on the hilltop of Monte alle Croci is the easiest way to grasp the full beauty of Florence. Not only does it offer the visitor a view of the city with its incomparable skyline spread out below – but the church itself, with the classic beauty of its finely articulated 12th–13th c. marble façade and priceless works of art in the interior, is one of the most beautiful and individual Romanesque churches in Italy.
There was probably a church here in the time of Charlemagne; Bishop Hildebrand ordered its renovation in 1018 and by the early 13th c. both building work and decoration were largely completed. The church, together with the monastery, was originally for Benedictine nuns but between 1373 and 1552 it was used by Olivetan monks who have recently been reinstated.

San Miniato al Monte: its impressively articulated façade

Mosaic in the apse: Christ with Mary and San Miniato

The plain aisled interior is one of the finest in the world. The architectural features – from inlaid floor to the painted beams of the roof, the columns and vaulting, alternating green and white marble and pleasing proportions – all combine in the form of a harmonious whole.

Interior

Left aisle
In the left aisle is the Cappella del Cardinale di Portogallo (or "di San Jacopo"), one of the most richly decorated and harmonious rooms of Florentine Renaissance architecture. Its outstanding works of art are the ceiling by Luca della Robbia, the tomb of the Cardinal-Archbishop Jacobo of Lisbon (hence the name of "the Cardinal of Portugal") by Rossellino (1461), two "flying angels" by the Pollaiolo brothers (1467), Baldovinetti's panel of the "Annunciation" and his two "Prophets" (1466–7).

Campanile
In the troubled early 16th c. San Miniato's Campanile was used to defend the people of Florence against the troops of the Emperor when Michelangelo mounted two cannon here during the siege of 1530. To the right of the church stands the huge Bishops' Palace (completed in 1320 but enlarged later); amidst the fortifications ("Fortezza") lies the vast cemetery, "Cimitero delle Porte Sante".

Nave
In the middle of the nave is the graceful chapel, the Cappella del Crocifisso, built by Michelozzo (1448) for Piero de' Medici. Its coffered ceiling is by Luca della Robbia, and Agnola Gaddi was responsible for the paintings.

Crypt
Steps on the right and the left lead down into the crypt, with six
rows of beautiful columns, groined vaulting and frescoes by
Taddeo Gaddi.

Presbytery and apse
The marble lattice-work (1207), the pulpit with the eagle of St
John under the lectern and the (restored) apse mosaic ("Christ
between the Virgin and St Minias") are among the notable
features in the presbytery and apse.

Sacristy
On the S side of the raised apse is the sacristy (1387) with
Spinello Aretino's masterpiece, "The Life of St Benedict". From
the sacristy a door leads into the cloister which has frescoes by
Andrea del Castagno and Paolo Uccello.

San Niccolò sopr'Arno (Church)   K7

Location
Via San Niccolò

Buses
B, 13n, 23r

An aedicula (built-up altar) in the style of Michelozzo and a
lively fresco, "Madonna della Cintola" by Piero del Pollaiolo
(1450) in the sacristy are the principal art treasures of the
church of San Niccolò sopr'Arno which was built in the 12th c.,
transformed in the 14th c. and restored in the 16th c.

San Pancrazio e Cappella Rucellai   H6
(Former Church and Rucellai Chapel)

Location
Via della Spada

The former church of San Pancrazio (now occupied by national
institutions) is worth seeing for its beautiful 14th c. façade and
for architectural features indicative of the work of the architect
Alberti.
Next to it is the Cappella Rucellai in which Leon Battista Alberti
was commissioned about the year 1467 by Giovanni Rucellai
to build a most unusual sepulchre which he modelled on the
Holy Sepulchre in Jerusalem.

San Salvatore al Monte (Or San Francesco al Monte; Church)   L7

Location
Above Piazzale
Michelangelo, Viale Galileo

Bus
13

The church of San Salvatore al Monte (or San Francesco al
Monte) tends to get overlooked because of the nearby church
of San Miniato (see entry) but the church that Michelangelo
called "la bella villanella" ("the beautiful country lass") is
worth visiting for its outstanding clearcut architecture both
inside and out. This is mainly the work of Cronaca (from 1499),
who had considerable difficulties to overcome. Because of the
steepness of the site building could proceed only by making
use of retaining walls.

San Simone (Church)   K6

Location
Piazza San Simone,
Via Isola della
Stinche

Restoration work after the 1966 floods revealed the extent
of the treasures that the little church of San Simone had to
offer. Founded in the 12th c. and completely transformed in the
17th c. by Silvani it has extremely elegant architecture and

valuable frescoes and paintings that had almost been forgotten, including a "St Peter in Majesty" ascribed to the "Master of St Cecilia" ("Maestro della S. Cecilia").

Sant'Ambrogio (Church) L6

St Ambrose is one of the oldest churches in Florence. The building was transformed at the end of the 13th c. and restored several times during the following centuries; the neo-Gothic façade was added in 1887.

The single-naved church contains the tombs of famous Renaissance artists, including Cronaca (d. 1580), Mino da Fiesole (d. 1484) and Verrocchio (d. 1488).

It is furnished with notable paintings and frescoes, among them the "Madonna del Latte" by Nardo di Cione, a triptych by Bicci di Lorenzo and Cosimo Rosselli's fresco of a "Procession".

A marble tabernacle by Mino da Fiesole (1481–3) in the Cappella del Miracolo (Chapel of the Miracle) depicts the event after which the chapel is named. In 1230 a priest failed to dry the chalice properly; the next morning, it is said, the wine had changed into blood.

Location
Piazza Sant'Ambrogio

**Santa Croce con Cappella dei Pazzi e Museo dell'Opera di Santa Croce K/L6
(Church of Santa Croce with Pazzi Chapel and Croce Museum)

"Santa Croce is a pantheon of the most dignified kind. The church has a serious and a gloomy solemnity, indeed it is a huge mortuary that no thinking person will enter without reverence", wrote Ferdinand Gregorovius, a German who travelled widely in Italy in the 19th c. It is a feeling shared by the visitor on approaching the church and entering its vast interior (photo on p. 119).

The largest and most beautiful of the Franciscan churches, Santa Croce was rebuilt in 1294 on the site of a chapel founded by St Francis of Assisi (possibly by Arnolfo di Cambio) and dedicated in 1443 in the presence of Pope Eugene IV. The façade, articulated in multicoloured marble, and the Campanile date from the 19th c.

Location
Piazza Santa Croce

Buses
13r, 14, 19n, 23, 31, 32, 33

Despite additions and restoration work the church, which has always been Franciscan, has retained the character of a medieval Gothic basilica. With its tombs and monuments (276 tombstones set in the floor) and numerous important works of art, it is one of the finest buildings in Italy and its importance is emphasised by its impressive size. It is 378·61 ft (115·43 m) long, the nave is 125.39 ft (38·23 m) wide and the transept 241·87 ft (73·74 m) wide.

The aisled interior with an open painted timber ceiling, octagonal columns supporting broad arches and stained-glass windows (placed there between 1320 and 1450) provides a solemn setting not only for the works of art but also for the services and sermons of the Franciscan monks.

Walking round the church in a clockwise direction the visitor should make a point of seeing the following:

Interior

117

N aisle

Opposite the first pillar is the tomb of the famous scientist Galileo Galilei (by Giulio Foggini). The monument to Carlo Marsuppini (by Desiderio da Settignano), one of the finest 15th c. monuments, is on the right of the side door.

N transept

On the left is the interesting monument to the Florentine composer Luigi Cherubini (d. 1842).

The Cappella Bardi in the centre contains Donatello's "Christ Crucified" which was criticised by Brunelleschi who maintained that Donatella had hung a peasant on the Cross. Brunelleschi himself created a more beautiful Crucifixion - or so he hoped – for Santa Maria Novella (see entry).

The N transept is rounded off by five chapels along the E wall. The Cappella Bardi di Vernio has wall frescoes with scenes from the life of St Sylvester (1340; by Maso di Banco); the frescoes in the burial recesses are by Maso di Banco and Taddeo Gaddi.

The Cappella Tosinghi-Spinelli has interesting stained-glass windows by the school of Giotto.

Apse

The apse is completely covered with frescoes. The frescoes in the vault are by Agnolo Gaddi (1380) and show the "Risen Christ, the Evangelists and St Francis". The wall frescoes, by Gaddi and his assistants, are of the Legend of the Cross.

S transept

The S transept also has five chapels along its E wall. The Cappella Bardi is notable for Giotto's frescoes representing the history of St Francis, which are numbered among Giotto's most mature and important works.

There are also remarkable frescoes by Giotto in the adjacent Cappella Peruzzi of scenes from the life of St John the Evangelist (right-hand wall) and of St John the Baptist (left-hand wall). These were particularly admired by the Renaissance painters and closely studied by Masaccio and Michelangelo.

In the last chapel on the left, the Cappella Velluti, are some damaged frescoes by a pupil of Cimabue ("Archangel Michael") and Giotto's "Coronation of the Virgin".

The door leads into the sacristy.

At the end of the transept is the Cappella Baroncelli with the family tomb (1328). The frescoes of the prophets at the entrance and the frescoes of the Life of the Virgin on the walls of the chapel are the greatest works of Taddeo Gaddi, one of Giotto's pupils.

In the adjoining Cappella Castellani there are important frescoes (Lives of the Saints) by Angelo Gaddi and his pupils and a beautiful tabernacle by Mino da Fiesole.

Sacristy

The doorway (by Michelozzo) gives on to a corridor, also by Michelozzo, which leads to the Sacristy. This contains fine Renaissance cabinets and a "Crucifixion" by Taddeo Gaddi.

At the back of the Sacristy is the 14th c. Cappella Rinuccini, covered with frescoes by Giovanni da Milano. At the end of the

View of the basilica of Santa Croce ▶

sacristy corridor is the Cappella del Noviziato (or dei Medici) which Michelozzo built for Cosimo the Elder in 1445. The altarpiece in terracotta, "Madonna and Child" (1480), is by Andrea della Robbia.

On the way back to the entrance can be seen:

S aisle
The tomb of the composer Gioacchino Rossini (d. 1868) and that of the Florentine politician Leonardo Bruni (d. 1444) by Bernardo Rossellino, the first Renaissance tomb in Florence. In a recess is the delicate relief of the Annunciation by Donatello (1435).
About half-way along the aisle is the tomb of Niccolò Machiavelli (d. 1527), the great historian and politician, by Spinazzi (1787).
On the fifth pillar is the octagonal marble pulpit by Benedetto da Maiano (1472–6) with scenes from the life of St Francis and allegorical figures.
Nearer the door is the monumental cenotaph of Dante (1829), Florence's tribute to the memory of the poet it had sent into exile and who died in Ravenna in 1321.
On the pillar nearest the door, above the stoup, is a relief by Antonio Rossellino, "Madonna del Latte" (1478) and, in front, the Tomb of Michelangelo (d. 1564) by Vasari (1570).

Convent of Santa Croce   On the right of the church is the entrance to the late 14th/early 15th c. conventual buildings of Santa Croce.

First cloister
This cloister was flooded in 1966 to a depth of 19·2 ft (5·85 m) which meant that restoration work was necessary.

Pazzi Chapel (see below)

Museo dell'Opera di S. Croce (see p. 122)

Great Cloister
This was designed by Brunelleschi and built after his death.

* Capella dei Pazzi (Pazzi Chapel)

Opening times
Mon.–Sat. 9 a.m.–5 p.m.;
Sun. and public holidays
9 a.m.–noon

The Pazzi Chapel is an independent complex within the church and convent of Santa Croce. It owes its fame to the architectural genius of Brunelleschi. He spent the period from 1430 (or 1443) until his death in 1446 working on this classic early-Renaissance building for Andrea de' Pazzi. It was to be the funerary chapel of the Pazzi family and the chapter-house of the Franciscan monks of Santa Croce.

First Cloister
The view from the first cloister of the monastery of Santa Croce reveals the harmony of the chapel exterior with its colonnade and cupola. The architrave of the porch is adorned with a frieze of small medallions bearing the heads of angels (Desiderio da Settignano) and the cupola has beautiful rosettes by Luca della Robbia who also carved the "Relief of St Andrew" (1445) above the wooden doors (by Giuliano da Sangallo; 1470–8).

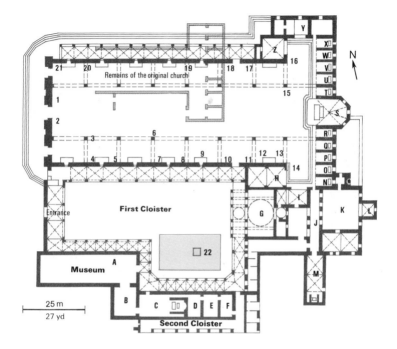

Santa Croce

Interior of the Gothic basilica

Interior
The interior, clearly articulated by pilasters, indentations, curvatures and barrel vault, gives the impression of uniformity, although the presence of the chancel means that the chapel is not rectangular. The four terracotta medallions in the spandrels, showing the seated Evangelists, are by Luca della Robbia, as are the twelve roundels of the Apostles (white ceramic on a blue ground).

*Museo dell'Opera di Santa Croce (Santa Croce Museum)

Opening times
Mon.–Sat. 9 a.m.–5 p.m.;
Sun. and public holidays
9 a.m.–noon

The museum is housed in the refectory of the monastery of Santa Croce. The particularly serious damage it suffered in the 1966 floods could only be put right by slow and painstaking restoration of the paintings, frescoes and statues.
Among the most important works of art are Taddeo Gaddi's huge (1291 sq. ft – 120 sq. m) "Last Supper", his "Entombment" and other pictures of the saints.
Other notable works include a "Crucifixion" by Cimabue, one of his later masterpieces, unfortunately seriously damaged, a bronze statue by Donatello, "St Louis" (1423), a fresco by Domenico Veneziano, "St John the Baptist and St Francis", Maso di Banco's "Coronation of the Virgin", and "Stigmata", a terracotta by Andrea della Robbia.

Sanata Felicità (Church)·   J6

Location
Piazza Santa Felicità

The church of Santa Felicità was built over an early Christian cemetery, rebuilt in the 11th and 14th c. and completely transformed in the 18th c. However, the porch and Vasari's "corridor", which passes through here on its way between the Palazzo degli Uffizi (see entry) and the Palazzo Pitti (see entry), were retained.

Above the entrance door is the box pew for the Grand Dukes who attended the services here.

To the right of the entrance in the Cappella Capponi can be found the church's most important works of art, two masterpieces by Pontormo (1526–8), "Entombment of Christ" and "Annunciation". The chapel was built by Brunelleschi for the Barbadori family.

The monastery belonging to the church is also of architectural interest (chapter-house).

Santa Lucia dei Magnoli   J/K7

The little church of Santa Lucia dei Magnoli is nicknamed "fra le rovinate" ("amidst the ruins") because the boulders on the hill were a danger to the houses surrounding it. It houses a beautiful panel by Lorenzetti of "Santa Lucia" painted on a gold ground.

Location
Via dei Bardi

Buses
B, 13n, 23r

Santa Margherita a Montici

The partly medieval church of Santa Margherita a Montici in the lovely Tuscan hills S of Florence (beyond Pian dei Giullari) has several fine works of art: the panels "Madonna" and "Santa Margherita" by the Master of St Cecilia (early 14th c.), "Madonna della Cintola" by Piero del Pollaiolo (1450), an altar in the style of Michelozzo, and finely worked 15th c. liturgical vestments.

Location
Via Pian dei Giullari, 2½ miles (4 km) S of the Porta San Giorgio

Bus
38

Santa Margherita de' Ricci   K6

In the centre of the city stands the church of Santa Margherita in Santa Maria de' Ricci or della Madonna de' Ricci which owes its name and its existence (1508) to the miraculous picture of the "Madonna de' Ricci" (c. 1300) on the high altar. Santa Margherita was the parish church of some well-known Florentine families.

Location
Via del Corso 6

Buses
14, 19n, 23, 31, 32, 33

Santa Maria del Carmine e Cappella Brancacci   G/H6
(Church and Brancacci Chapel)

The large church stands in the Piazza of the same name in a busy working-class quarter of Florence. The church, begun in 1268, was not completed until 1476, as can be seen from the fact that there are both Romanesque and Gothic elements along the sides. Transformed in the 16th and 17th c., it was so badly damaged by fire in 1771 that it had to be rebuilt (by Ruggieri and Mannaioni, until 1782). The ground plan of the church is a Latin cross with a single nave flanked by various chapels. It is adjoined on the right by a cloister built in the early 17th c.

The church is principally famed for the Brancacci Chapel which houses frescoes by Masaccio (end of the right arm of the

Location
Piazza del Carmine

Buses
6, 11, 36, 37

transept) and for the Baroque Cappella Corsini by Pierfrancesco Silvani (1675–83; left arm of transept), with, in the dome, a fresco of the "Apotheosis of St Andrea Corsini" by Luca Giordano (1682). The chapel contains the tombs of Neri and Pietro Corsini with three high-reliefs in marble by Giovanni Battista Foggini.

*Cappella Brancacci (Brancacci Chapel)

Location
Piazza del Carmine

Opening times
9 a.m.–noon and 3.30–
6 p.m. daily

In 1428 Felice Brancacci, a wealthy Florentine merchant and politician, commissioned painters, principally Masaccio and Masolino, to decorate the Brancacci family chapel with frescoes which represented an important stage in the development of European painting. In his frescoes Masaccio took art beyond the richness of form and colour of the medieval Gothic and developed the ideas initiated by the famous painter Giotto. Major Renaissance artists studied the works in the Brancacci Chapel on account of their confidence in the use of perspective, the austere realism of the characters depicted, the subtle characterisation of the faces, the freedom and intensity of expression.

In this Masaccio surpassed Masolino, 18 years his senior.

Following both traditions Filippino Lippi painted the lower row of five frescoes.

The themes of the frescoes are (top row, from left to right): Expulsion of Adam and Eve from Paradise, The Tribute Money (both masterpieces by Masaccio); St Peter Preaching; Peter Baptising the Neophytes; Peter and John Healing the Lame and Raising Tabitha; The Temptation of Adam and Eve.

Bottom row: Peter Visited by Paul in Prison; Peter Raising the Son of Theophilus; Peter Preaching; Peter (with John) Healing the Sick; Peter and John Distributing Alms; Crucifixion of Peter; Peter and Paul before the Proconsul; Release of Peter from Prison.

▼ *Fresco by Masaccio in the Cappella Brancacci: The Tribute Money*

Michelangelo is said to have become so enraged during an argument on the steps of the church while discussing these pictures that he got his nose broken in the ensuing fisticuffs.

Santa Maria dell'Impruneta

The 11th c. basilica stands in the little town of Impruneta which nestles among the hills of Tuscany. It was rebuilt in the 14th and 15th c. and surrounded by walls and towers. The church was severely damaged during the Second World War (photo page 126).

Of interest inside are two richly decorated aediculae by Michelozzo (1453–6), similar to the one in the church of Santissima Annunziata (see entry) in Florence, the Cappella della Croce with an altarpiece by Luca della Robbia, and the Cappella della Madonna, also decorated with works by Luca della Robbia.

The little town of Impruneta is well-known for its pottery and ceramics. The annual Fiera di San Luca is celebrated in October.

Location
Impruneta, 8 miles
(13 km) S

*Santa Maria Maddalena dei Pazzi,   K5
Convento di S. Maria Maddalena (Church and Convent)

Maria Maddalena, a member of the famous Florentine Pazzi family, was canonised in 1669. The 13th c. complex of church and Benedictine convent, already transformed two centuries earlier by Giuliano da Sangallo (1480–92), was enlarged in her honour, which is why the forecourt of the church is in the harmonious style of the second half of the 15th c. and yet there are Baroque elements in other sections of the church and the convent.

In the chapels are some valuable paintings by 15th and 16th c. artists (e.g. Portelli and Giordano).

Location
Borgo Pinti 58

Buses
6, 13r, 14, 19r, 23, 31, 32, 33, 34

Santa Maria Maddalena dei Pazzi

Santa Maria dell'Impruneta

Santa Marie dei Pazzi: Benedictine church

Convento di Santa Maria Maddalena

In the chapter-house of the convent adjoining the church is one of Perugino's finest frescoes, dating from between 1493 and 1496, his most creative period: Christ on the Cross and Mary Magdalene, St Bernard and Mary, St John and Benedict, Christ on the Cross Helping St Bernard.

In the background the landscape is recognisably that of Perugino's native Umbria (Perugia).

The convent's refectory is today part of a Carabinieri barracks; Sangallo's cloister belongs to the Liceo Michelangelo. Most of the damage caused by the 1966 flooding has been repaired.

Opening times
10 a.m.–4 p.m. daily (ring if closed)

Santa Maria Maggiore (Church)   J5

Not far from the Baptistery (see Battistero), in Via de' Cerretani, is one of the oldest churches in Florence, which was certainly built before the 11th c. and was rebuilt in the second half of the 13th c. (1912–13 carefully restored). The old bell-tower is still indicative of the lower level of the Romanesque church; high up in the wall is "Bertha", a late-Romanesque bust of a woman. Above the church portal is the "Madonna and Child" of the 14th c. Pisan school (copy).

The outstanding features of the aisled Gothic interior with its square pillars and fine paintings and statues are the "Madonna in Majesty with Child" (also known as "Madonna del Carmelo") and a coloured gilded wooden relief. The relief shows the artist's skill not only as a sculptor but also as a painter (possibly Coppo di Marcovaldo, 13th c.).

Location
Via de' Cerretani

Buses
B, 1, 4, 6, 7, 10, 11, 14, 17, 19, 23, 31, 32

**Santa Maria Novella (Church)   H5

One of the most important churches in Florence, the Dominican church of Santa Maria Novella was built in 1246 on the site of a 10th c. oratory (Santa Maria delle Vigne) and continually enlarged between the 11th and the 14th c. by various architects (essentially completed about 1360).

Like the Franciscan church of Santa Croce (see entry), the approach to the main building is across a large square (see Piazza di Santa Maria Novella. Here the façade is articulated by coloured marble. It was added between 1456 and 1470 by Leon Battista Alberti on the orders of Giovanni Rucellai (whose family crest, the billowing sails, form the architrave half way up). The architect gave it its distinctive shape by combining Romanesque-Gothic and Renaissance styles (portal, pillars on either side, design of the upper section).

To the right of the church is an old cemetery.

The interior of the church displays a harmonious balance between soaring Gothic shapes and the extensive uniform nave which appears even longer than it is (325·5 ft – 99·2 m) because the bays decrease in width from 49·2 ft (15 m) down to 37·4 ft (11·4 m) as they approach the altar. The width of 93·2 ft (28·4 m) (201·94 ft – 61·4 m in the transept) lends the Gothic interior an air of solidly based integrity.

Location
Piazza di Santa Maria Novella

Buses
9, 13, 14, 17, 19, 22, 23, 36, 37

Opening times
Mon.–Thurs., Sat. 9 a.m.–2 p.m.; Sun. and public holidays 8 a.m.–1 p.m.

Closed
Fri.

Interior

Santa Maria Novella: one of the most important Florentine churches

Walking clockwise round the church the visitor can see the following important works of art:

Entrance
In the lunette above the portal is a fresco of the "Nativity" (after Filippo Lippi); in the rose-window, the oldest in Florence, the "Coronation of the Virgin".

Left aisle
On the second pillar is a marble pulpit by Buggiano from designs by Brunelleschi. On the third altar is the "Trinity", a fresco by Masaccio (1427), considered to be one of his finest works on account of its intensity of expression and perfect perspective.

Sacristy
A door leads into the sacristy which contains a marble lavabo (Giovanni della Robbia) and a "Crucifixion" by Giotto (above the door).

Left arm of the transept
Nardo di Cione painted the frescoes (based on Dante's "Divine Comedy") in the raised Cappella Strozzi in 1357. The chapel also contains Andrea Orcagna's altarpiece, "Redeemer and Saints".

A striking feature of the Cappella Gaddi is Bronzino's painting above the altar of "Christ raising the Daughter of Jairus".
In the adjacent Cappella Gondo is the celebrated wooden crucifix (between 1410 and 1425) carved by Brunelleschi in response to Donatello's crucifix in Santa Croce (see entry).

Apse
The apse was completely covered in frescoes by Domenico Ghirlandaio and his assistants (scenes from the life of John the Baptist and the Virgin). The bronze crucifix is by Giambologna.

Right arm of the transept
This also has two chapels on the left-hand side. The Cappella di Filippo Strozzi, the church's principal founder, is decorated with frescoes by Filippino Lippi (1497–1502). The Cappella dei Bardi houses Vasari's "Rosary Madonna" (1570).
At the end of the transept is the Cappella Rucellai with the bronze plate marking the grave of the Dominican-General Dati by Lorenzo Ghiberti (1423) and a marble statue of "Madonna and Child" by Nini Pisano. Nearby, in the wall opposite the chapels, is the tomb of Joseph, Patriarch of Constantinople, who died here in 1440 after the Council of Florence.

Right aisle
Here a door leads into the Cappella della Pura with the miraculous picture of "Madonna and Child and St Catherine". Centred around this picture is the legend that in 1472 the Virgin, speaking from out of the picture, told two grubby children that they needed to wash themselves, an event much appreciated by Florentine mothers in bringing up their children. The chapel leads into the old cemetery.
Nearer the entrance are the tomb of the Beata Villana by Rossellino (1451) and the side altar with Macchietti's "Martyrdom of St Laurence" (1573).

A visit to Santa Maria Novella should also include the cloisters and the adjoining chapels of the former monastery of Santa Maria Novella (entrance to the left of the façade).

Cloisters and monastery chapels

"Chiostro Verde"
The name "Green Cloister" refers to the green tones of frescoes by Paolo Uccello of scenes from the Old Testament which are badly damaged, and of which the "Flood" and the "Sacrifice of Noah" are the masterpieces.

Refectory
Paolo Uccello's masterpieces "The Flood" and "Noah's Sacrifice".

Great Cloister
With special permission it is possible to visit from here the Cappella dei Papi on the first floor which has frescoes by Pontormo.

Cappellone degli Spagnoli
The "Spanish Chapel" was built after 1340 by Jacopo Talenti as the chapter-house of the Dominican monastery and assigned in 1540 by Eleonora of Toledo, wife of Cosimo I, to her Spanish retainers (hence the name) as a place of worship. Its frescoes are among 14th c. Italy's greatest paintings.
Andrea da Firenze (Bonaiuti) was given the theme for his paintings – "the Dominican Order and the new open path to Salvation" – by Prior Jacopo Passavanti, and combined scenes from the Scriptures, legends of saints and allegories of the Humanities.

These paintings serve as a tribute to the culture of the 14th c. in a similar way to Raphael's celebration of 16th c. culture in his Stanze frescoes in the Vatican.

Chiostrino dei Morti
The tour ends with a visit to the "Little Cloister of the Dead" with the Strozzi funerary chapel (Cappella funeraria degli Strozzi).

---

*Santa Trinità (Church)   J6

Location
Piazza Santa Trinità

Buses
A, B, 6, 11

The fondness of the Florentines for the church of Santa Trinità is due mainly to its venerable age. As early as the 11th c. there was a church here which was rebuilt in the 13th c. (probably by Nicola Pisano) as the first Gothic church in Florence. It was rebuilt once again in the second half of the 14th c., this time by Neri di Fioravante. The Baroque façade by Buontalenti (1593–4) is therefore in complete contrast to the soaring style of the Gothic interior.

Interior

It has many notable works of art (here listed clockwise):

Left aisle
In the third chapel an "Annunciation" on a gold ground by Neri di Bicci and the tomb of Giuliano Davanzati (d. 1444), an early Christian sarcophagus with high reliefs; in the fifth chapel Mary Magdalene in wood by Desiderio da Settignano and Benedetto da Maiano (1464–5).

Left arm of the transept
In the left arm of the transept is the marble tomb of Bishop Benozzi Federighi (1455–6), one of Luca della Robbia's finest works.

Right arm of the transept
In the right arm of the transept the Cappella Sassetti has celebrated frescoes by Domenico Ghirlandaio (1483–6) of the "Life of St Francis" (including the famous "Confirmation of the Rule of the Order") into which the artist incorporated contemporary personalities and buildings such as Lorenzo the Magnificent, Ghirlandaio himself, hand on hip, and the Piazza della Signoria and Piazza della Trinità. The altarpiece "Adoration of the Shepherds" is also by Ghirlandaio (1485).

Sacristy
In the sacristy is the tomb of Onofrio Strozzi by Piero di Niccolò Lamberti (1421).

Right aisle
There is a cycle of frescoes by Lorenzo Monaco in the Cappella Salimbeni and a 14th c. "Crucifixion" on panel in the chapel nearest the entrance.

Nave
Stairs in the middle of the nave lead down to the old Romanesque church below.

*Santi Apostoli (Church)   J6

According to an inscription in Latin (on the left of the façade) the "Church of the Holy Apostles" was founded by Charlemagne and dedicated by Archbishop Turpinus. All that is known for certain is that the church was in existence at the end of the 11th c. and was rebuilt in the 15th and 16th c. (restored between 1930 and 1938). Benedetto da Rovezzano added a fine portal to the Romanesque façade in the early 16th c.

The columns of green marble from Prato with composite capitals (the first two from the nearby Roman baths) which separate the aisles from the nave constitute a striking feature of the interior. The church and its works of art were severely damaged in the 1966 floods.

Particularly noteworthy are, in the left aisle, a large terracotta tabernacle by Giovanni della Robbia (presbytery) and the tomb of Oddo Altaviti by Benedetto da Rovezzano (1507); and, in the right aisle, a panel by Vasari "Immaculate Conception" (1541, third chapel).

Location
Borgo Santi Apostoli

Bus
B

**Santissima Annunziata (Church of the Annunciation)   K5

Whereas the Cathedral (see Duomo Santa Maria del Fiore) serves as the eccesiastical-religious centre of Florence and the Palazzo Vecchio (or Palazzo della Signoria; see Palazzo Vecchio) is the secular-political centre, it is, quite rightly, the square and church of Santissima Annunziata that constitute the intellectual focal point of the city. Clustered around the square are the Spedale degli Innocenti and the Pinacoteca dello Spedale, Santa Maria degli Innocenti, the nearby university with its various faculties, the Museo di San Marco (see San Marco), the Galleria dell'Accademia (see entry) and the Accademia delle Belle Arti.

The church of the Annunziata, founded about 1250 as an oratory for the Servite Order and completely rebuilt between 1444 and 1481 by Michelozzo, is an architectural masterpiece, not least because of the unusual ground plan for the church and its monastry (nave with side chapels and a large round choir chapel in front, all with adjoining structures), while the church also houses many superb works of art.

Location
Piazza della SS. Annunziata

Buses
B, 1, 4, 6, 7, 10, 11, 17, 25

Portico
Four doors open out of the seven-arched portico which is supported by columns with elegant Corinthian capitals.

The door on the left leads past the Sagrestia della Madonna to the Chiostro dei Morti (Cloister of the Dead) with its fresco of "Madonna del Sacco" (after the bag against which St Joseph is leaning), one of the major works of Andrea del Sarto (1525). Adjoining the Chiostro dei Morti are the chapter-house, the Cappella della Confraternità di San Luca, the "Chapel of the Crucified", the relic chapel and the sacristy.

The right-hand door leads to the Cappella Pucci or di San Sebastiano, and the two middle doors to the Chiostrino dei Voti ("Little Cloister of the Votive Offerings" after the votive offerings hung here by the faithful), the atrium built by Manetti (1447) to designs by Michelozzo.

Exterior

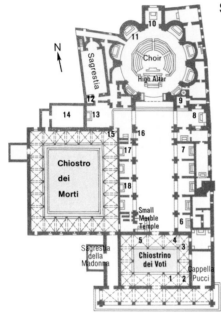

Santissima Annunziata

1 "Assunzione", by Rosso Fiorentino
2 "Visitazione", by Pontormo
3 "Natività di Maria", by Andrea del Sarto (1514)
4 "Arrivo dei Magi", by Andrea del Sarto (1511)
5 "Natività", by A. Baldovinetti (1460–62)
6 "Madonna in gloria, San Niccolò e Santi", by Empoli
7 Monument to Orlando de' Medici, by B. Rossellino
8 Cappella del Sacramento
9 Pietà, by B. Bandinelli (1559)
10 Cappella della Madonna del Soccorso, partly by Giambologna
11 "Resurrezione", by Bronzino, and wooden statue of St Roch, by Veit Stoss
12 Cappellina delle Reliquie
13 Cappella del Crocifisso
14 Cappella della Confraternità di San Luca
15 "Madonna del Sacco", by Andrea del Sarto
16 Organ dating from 1628
17 "Assunzione", by Perugino
18 "Santissima Trinità", fresco, by A. del Castagno (1454–5)

Chiostrino dei Voti

The early 16th c. frescoes in this atrium are famous. From left to right there are masterpieces by Andrea del Sarto (scenes from the life of St Filippo Benizzi); Cosimo Rosselli ("Vocation and Investiture of St Filippo Benizzi", 1476); Alesso Baldovinetto ("Nativity", 1460–2); another two by Andrea del Sarto ("Coming of the Magi" and, one of the artist's best works, "Birth of the Virgin", 1514) and Franciabigi's "Marriage of the Virgin", 1513, spoiled by the artist himself who destroyed Mary's head because the monks looked at the picture before its completion.

Finally there are more masterpieces by Pontormo ("Visitation of Mary", 1516) and Rosso Fiorentino ("Assumption of the Virgin", 1517).

Interior

Inside to the left of the entrance is a large marble tabernacle built at the behest of Piero de' Medici from a design by Michelozzo for the miraculous picture of the Annunciation of which there are many copies in Italy. It is said that the monk who was painting this picture in the 13th c. fell asleep out of despondency at his lack of skill when it came to depicting a wondrously fair Madonna and Mary's face was completed by an angel. Florentine newly-weds still come here and the bride leaves her bouquet by the Madonna.

The chapels are richly decorated with paintings and statues. The Following are the most interesting (clockwise):

Left side
In the left aisle is the Cappella Feroni which contains a fresco by Andrea del Castagno, "Redeemer and St Julian" (1455). The second chapel also has a fresco by Castagno, "Holy Trinity", one of his last highly realistic works. In the fourth chapel is a panel by Perugino, "Ascension of Christ".

Tribuna
Michelozzo began building the Tribuna, a rotunda divided into nine chapels, in 1451 and Leon Battista Alberti completed it to a different design. The fourth chapel from the left contains a painting by Angelo Bronzino, "Resurrection" (1550). The Cappella della Madonna del Soccorso (Madonna of Succour) was designed by Giambologna between 1594 and 1598 as his own tomb and is richly adorned with frescoes, statues and reliefs.

Dome
The dome is decorated with a fresco showing the Coronation of the Virgin by Volterrano (1681–3).

Right arm of the transept
Just inside the first chapel is a lovely "Pietà" by Baccio Bandinelli who is buried here with his wife.

**Santo Spirito (Church)   H6

Several wealthy Florentine families joined forces in the early years of the 15th c. to build a new church on the site of one that had been burnt down. They commissioned Brunelleschi, the city's famous architect, to design it. At the time of his death (1446) building work had progressed as far as the vaulting, but then it practically came to a standstill under various architects (bell-tower: Baccio d'Agnolo, 1503–17) and was never completed wholly in accordance with the original plans. This is why the austere exterior of the building shown no hint that Santo Spirito is one of the most purely Renaissance churches. The façade of the church, which was consecrated in 1481, was executed in the 18th c. and is of bare plaster without ornamentation. It is characterised by its outline and the large round window in the middle. The façade has doors of different sizes corresponding to the nave and two aisles inside.

Location
Piazza Santo Spirito

Buses
A, B

The interior is thought to be one of the most brilliant creations of the Florentine Renaissance. The plan is a Latin cross 318 ft (97 m) long, 108 ft (32 m) wide (transept 190 ft (58 m) wide) with a colonnaded central nave and side aisles and, built into the surrounding walls, forty semicircular side chapels. Its many works of art, tombs and monuments make Santo Spirito an impressive museum.
The side altars are resplendent with painting and statues, reliefs and liturgical objects. The visitor will find the following works of art of particular interest:

Interior

The rose-window in the façade was designed by Perugino ("Descent of the Holy Ghost"). The most important work in the church, "Madonna and Child with Saints and Donors", by Filippino Lippi (1490), is in the right arm of the transept, as is

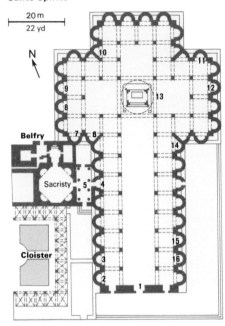

20 m
22 yd

N

Belfry

Sacristy

Cloister

Santo Spirito

1 Window, "Discesa dello Spirito Santo", after Perugino
2 "Resurrezione", by di Jacopo
3 "Christo Risorto", by Landini, copy after Michelangelo
4 Access to the sacristy
5 Cronaca's vestibule, designed by Sangallo
6 "Andata al Calvario", by M. Ghirlandaio
7 "Madonna col Bambino in trono e Santi", by dei Cari
8 "La Santissima Trinità adorata dalle Sante Caterina e Maddalena", by Granacci
9 Cappella Corbinelli, architecture and sculptures by Sansovino
10 "Presepio", by the school of Ghirlandaio
11 "Sposalizio della Vergine", by Sagrestani, and marble tomb of Neri di Gino Capponi
12 "Madonna col Bambino e San Giovannino", by F. Lippi
13 High altar by Caccini
14 "Raffaele e Tobiolo", marble panel, by Baratta (c. 1690)
15 San Nicola da Tolentino, wooden statue, by N. Unghero
16 Copy of Michelangelo's Pietà in Rome, by di Baccio Bigio (1549)

the marble sarcophagus of Neri di Gino Capponi, ascribed to Bernardo Rossellino (1458). On the left-hand side of the apse there is an "Annunciation" (15th c. Florentine school) and a devout 'Nativity" by the school of Ghirlandaio.

Sacristy
In the left-hand aisle is the entrance to a beautiful vestibule built by Cronaca (1492–4) with a door leading into the sacristy, an octagonal chamber designed by Giuliano da Sangallo (1495–6) and a masterpiece of European architecture.

Cloister
Another door in the vestibule leads into the first cloister, which is by Giulio and Alfonso Parigi (c. 1600). The second cloister, built by Ammanati between 1564 and 1569, is usually inaccessible because it is used for administrative purposes.

Left arm of the transept
It is worth having a look in the first chapel at Michele Ghirlandaio's painting, "Ascent of Calvary" and the glass in the window.
In the next chapel (moving clockwise) is Raffaele di Carli's panel, "Madonna in Majesty with Child" (1505).
In the second chapel along from this there is another panel, "Trinity worshipped by St Catherine and St Mary Magdalene", which is ascribed to Francesco Granacci.
Next door is the Cappella Corbinelli (sacramental chapel), exquisitely designed by Andrea Sansovino (1492), who was also responsible for the sculpture.

To the left of the church is the entrance to the Cenacolo di Santo Spirito. This refectory is all that remains of the old Augustinian monastery. It contains a large fresco of the Last Supper, attributed to Andrea Orcagna (c. 1360), which, though severely damaged, is one of the great 14th c. works of art in Florence. The refectory also houses the Salvatore Romano Foundation's fine sculptures.

Cenacolo di Santo Spirito

Opening times
Tues.–Sat. 9 a.m.–2 p.m.;
Sun. and public holidays
8 a.m.–1 p.m.

Closed
Mon.

---

* Santo Stefano al Ponte (Church)   J6

In a small traffic-free square, mentioned in documents as early as 1116, is the church of Santo Stefano al Ponte (or "Santi Stefano e Cecilia"). The ravages of the Second World War and the 1966 floods have been righted and once again the church displays the elements of the various centuries (13th c. façade, 16th c. altars, 17th c. nave renovation) in all their glory.
The bronze relief, "The Stoning of St Stephen" is the work of Ferdinando Tocca (1656). Buontalenti's impressive marble staircase (1574) leading to the presbytery was formerly in the church of Santa Trinità (see entry).

Location
Piazzeta Santo Stefano

Settignano

The Via Poggio to Settignano, a small town E of Florence, passes the villa where the company in Boccaccio's "Decamerone" sought refuge from the plague.
In San Martino a Mensola is the lovely church of the same name (with a triptych by Taddeo Gaddi) and not far from there is the villa known as "I Tatti", the headquarters, after the death in 1959 of the art critic Berenson, of Harvard University's Centre for Renaissance History. The "Collezione Berenson" contains valuable works of art.
Next comes the little Oratorio della Vannella, at Ponte a Mensola, and then Castello Vincigliata, the property of the Visdomini.
In Settignano it is worth paying a visit to the 15th c. parish church of the "Assunta", a building that has undergone several renovations. Nearby is the Villa Gamberaia, one of the finest villas of the 16th c. although damaged during the Second World War, where the gardens are extremely fine.

Bus
10

Location
5 miles (8 km) E

---

* Spedale degli Innocenti e Pinacoteca dello Spedale   K5
(Foundling Hospital and Art Gallery)

In 1419 the guild of silk merchants and tailors commissioned the architect Filippo Brunelleschi, who built the dome of the cathedral (see Duomo Santa Maria del Fiore), to build a foundling hospital. Abandoned children were called Innocenti (Innocents) in remembrance of the children murdered in Bethlehem. Mothers who wanted to bring their new-born babies to the orphanage anonymously could (until 1875) place them in a revolving wooden cylinder ("Ruota") at the end of the portico. The Spedale degli Innocenti marks the beginning of Renaissance architecture in Florence.

Location
Piazza della SS. Annunziata

Buses
1, 4 ,6, 7, 10, 11, 17, 25, 34

Times of opening
Tues.–Sat., Sun., public
holidays 9 a.m.–1 p.m.

Closed
Mon.

Loggia

The Spedale is famed for the harmonious colonnade of its loggia. The consummate architecture is complemented by frescoes under the arcades and in the lunettes above the doors, as well as by the ten famous terracotta medallions by Andrea della Robbia (*c.* 1463), each representing a baby in swaddling clothes.

Santa Maria degli Innocenti

The porch leads to the church of Santa Maria degli Innocenti with, beyond, a cloister designed by Brunelleschi connected by a door with the church. In the lunette is a terracotta "Annunciation" by Andrea della Robbia.

Collection of frescoes

Besides the Pinacoteca dello Spedale degli Innocenti collection there is also on the first floor a collection of detached fescoes that have been removed from their original locations. They are by Florentine artists including Poccetti, Bicci di Lorenzo, Lorenzo Monaco, Allori, Rosselli, Ghirlandaio, Fra Bartolommeo, Perugino and della Robbia.

*Pinacoteca dello Spedale degli Innocenti (art gallery)

Opening times
Tues.–Sat., Sun., public holidays 9 a.m.–1 p.m.

Closed
Mon.

The Pinacoteca has a collection of pictures, sculptures, miniatures and furniture dating from the 14th to the 18th c. Its most notable exhibits include works by Giovanni del Biondo, Rossellino and Benedetto da Maiano with those of Domenico Ghirlandaio and Andrea del Sarto as well as Luca della Robbia's terracotta "Madonna" meriting a special mention.

Uffizi

See Palazzo e Galleria degli Uffizi

Via Tornabuoni   J6

One of the most elegant (because of its shops), most beautiful (thanks to 19th c. planning) and most interesting (on account of its 15th–19th c. palaces) streets in Florence, the Via Tornabuoni is like a history book come to life, where the story of the city is made manifest in splendid buildings: Palazzi Larderel-Giacomini (early 16th c.), Corsi-Tornabuoni (1875, with a courtyard by Michelozzo that survived from the Palazzo Tornabuoni), Loggetta dei Tornaquinci (early 16th c.) and the Palazzo Strozzi (17th c.).

Ville Medicee

The Medici family and its many relatives had at its disposal three villas to the NW of the city in the beautiful hills of Tuscany which they used as summer residences – the villas of Careggi, Petraia and Castello. Here the architects could give free rein to their skills and imagination – though within the framework of Renaissance architecture – as they worked on the buildings and gardens, while the artists, painters and sculptors were presented with plenty of opportunities to display the lighter side of their art.

Via Tornabuoni: one of the most interesting streets in the city

Garden and Villa Medicea di Castello

Practical Information

Academies (Accademie)

Accademia Cappiello
Via Alfani 70, tel. 21 52 42

Accademia dei Georgofili
Loggiato degli Uffizi, tel. 21 33 60

Accademia dei Piccoli
Via Alfani 81, tel. 28 31 37

Accademia della Crusca
Via di Castello 46 (Villa Medicea), tel. 45 28 41

Accademia della Lingua Italiana Nicolò Machiavelli
(Cultural Institute for Foreigners)
Piazza Santo Spirito 4, tel. 29 69 66

Accademia della Signoria
Via Maggio 28, tel. 21 26 50

Accademia delle Arti del Disegno
Via Orsanmichele 4, tel. 26 08 34

Accademia di Belle Arti
Via Ricasoli 66, tel. 21 54 49
and Via Michelozzi 2, tel. 28 43 55

Accademia Fiorentina Billiardo
Via G. Capponi 18, tel. 21 32 62

Accademia Internazionale di Lingue
(School for Interpreters)
Via Bufalini 3, tel. 21 38 09

Accademia Italiana di Lotte Orientali
Viale Verga 23, tel. 61 07 13

Accademia Scuola per Corrispondenza
Via A. G. Dosio 58, tel. 71 09 90

Accademia Toscana di Scienze e Lettere "La Colombaria"
Via S. Egidio 23, tel. 29 66 28

Airlines

Alitalia
Lungarno Acciaiuoli 10/12r, tel. 26 30 51
Flight Reservations, tel. 27 88

British Airways
Via della Vigna Nuova 36/38r, tel. 21 86 55

Pan Am
Lungarno Acciaiuoli 4, tel. 28 27 16

TWA
Piazza S. Trinità 2, tel. 29 68 56

Airport

Florence does not have its own civil airport. National and international traffic for Florence passes through "Galileo Galilei" Airport near Pisa. There is a regular bus service between the airport and the main station in Florence (c. 53 miles – 85 km).

Antiques

Borgo Ognissanti, Via Maggio, Via Fossi, San Spirito are the streets with a particularly large number of antique shops.

Banks

Mon.–Fri. 9 a.m.–12.30 (closed in the afternoon).   Opening times

Most banks in the city centre will cash Eurocheques. Since each bank may quote a different rate it is worth while comparing them.   Eurocheques

Camping sites (Campeggi)

Parco Comunale   Florence
Viale Michelangelo 80, tel. 6 81 19 77
closed November–March
c. 500 pitches

Villa Camerata
Viale A. Righi 2/4, tel. 61 03 00
c. 180 pitches

Camping Park Albatros
Via Forte di San Giorgio 1/a, tel. 29 31 55

Camping Internazionale Firenze   Impruneta
Via San Cristoforo-Bottai 2, tel. 2 02 04 45

Camping Panoramico Fiesole   Fiesole
Via Peramonda, tel. 59 90 69

Detailed information concerning camping sites is given in the annually revised camping guide published by the AA.   Camping guide

Car Hire

Hertz	Via Maso Finiguerra 33, tel. 28 22 60 and 29 85 05 Hertz has desks at Peretola Airport and in the main railway station.
AVIS	Via Borgognissanti 128r, tel. 21 36 29 and 29 88 26
Europacar	Via Borgognissanti 120r, tel. 29 34 44 and 29 41 30
Information	See the yellow pages (Pagine Gialle) under "autonoleggio".

Chemists (Farmacie)

	All'Insegna di San Giovanni di Dio Borgognissanti 40r, tel. 27 08 77
Open at night	Codecà "Notturno" Via Ginori 50r, tel. 27 08 49
Opening times	Summer: Mon.–Fri. 8.30 a.m.–12.30, 4–8 p.m. Winter: Mon.–Fri. 8.30 a.m.–12.30, 3.30–7.30 p.m.
Information	Telephone 110 to find out about the nearest chemist that is open on Sundays.

Consulates

United Kingdom	Lungarno Corsini 2, tel.: 21 25 94

Currency

Currency	The unit of currency is the *lira* (plural *lire*). There are banknotes for 500, 1000, 2000, 5000, 10,000, 20,000, 50,000 and 100,000 lire and coins in denominations of 5, 10, 20, 50, 100 and 200 lire. There is often a shortage of small change, and telephone tokens (*gettoni*) or postage stamps may be used to make up the deficiency.
Import of currency	There are no restrictions on the import of foreign currency into Italy, but in view of the strict control on the export of currency it is advisable to declare any currency brought in on the appropriate form (*modulo V2*) at the frontier. There is a limit of 200,000 lire per head on the import of Italian currency.
Export of currency	The export of foreign currency is permitted only up to a value of 300,000 lire per person except where a larger sum has been declared on entry. No more than 200,000 litre of Italian currency can be taken out.
Travellers' cheques, etc.	It is advisable to take money in the form of travellers' cheques, which are not subject to any restrictions, or to use a Euro bank card. The principal credit cards are widely accepted.
Changing money	See Banks, p. 139

Customs regulations

Visitors to Italy can take in, without liability to duty, clothing, toilet articles, jewellery and other personal effects (including two cameras and a small ciné camera with 10 films each, camping equipment and sports gear), together with reasonable quantities of food for the journey. In addition visitors can take in the usual duty-free allowances of alcohol, tobacco and perfume (varying for EEC nationals, US visitors, other European citizens and overseas residents).

Visitors can take out, without liability to duty, articles they have bought in Italy up to a value of approx. 1,000,000 lire. For the export of objets d'art and antiques a permit must be obtained from the Chamber of Art.

Events

International handicraft fair (until May) Easter Sunday: Scoppio del Carro ("Explosion of the cart" in the Cathedral Square)	April
Ascension Day: Spring festival ("Festa del grillo") in the Parco delle Cascine Maggio Musicale Fiorentino: Music festival (until July)	May
24 June: Festival of St John the Baptist (patron saint of Florence) and fireworks	June
Other events during June: Firenze estate (Florentine summer): cultural and musical events Gioco del Calcio, revival of the football match in medieval costumes (in the Giardino di Boboli) Horse racing	
Football match in 16th c. costumes Horse racing	July
Musical and cultural events for tourists Pitti Bimbo (Fair of children's fashions) International leather goods fair	August
Pitti Uomo (Fair of men's fashions) Pitti Filate (Fair of knitwear, etc.) Casual (Fair of leisurewear fashions) Oltrarno di Firenze (September festival) Horse racing	September
Antiques Fair Horse racing Pitti Donna (Fair of women's fashions) International furniture show Exhibition of plants and flowers	October
Start of the opera, concert and theatre season Italian ophthalmic exhibition Horse racing	November

December	Christmas cribs (Nativity groups) in numerous locations

Excursions

	Excursions in the vicinity of Florence with multi-lingual guides can be booked at most travel agencies or hotels. From April to June there are also tours visiting the gardens of Florence's most beautiful villas. There are excursions to see farms and estates around Florence in September and October.
Reservation	These excursions and tours can be booked at the following addresses: C.I.T. Via Cerretani 57r, tel. 29 43 06 Piazza Stazione 51r, tel. 28 41 45
Travel agencies	See Travel agencies, p. 160

First aid

Ambulance	First aid, tel. 21 22 22
Guardia Medica	24-hour emergency ambulance service, tel. 47 78 91
Hospitals	See Hospitals, p. 144

Galleries (Gallerie)

Collezione Contini Bonacossi
Palazzo Pitti
Open: Tues.–Sat. 9 a.m.–2 p.m.; Sun., public holidays 9 a.m.–1 p.m.
Closed: Mon.

Galleria dell'Accademia
See A–Z

Galleria d'Arte Moderna
See A–Z, Palazzo Pitti

Galleria Corsini
See A–Z, Palazzo Corsini

Galleria Ferroni
See A–Z

Galleria Palatina
See A–Z, Palazzo Pitti

Galleria Strozzina
See A–Z, Palazzo Strozzi

Galleria degli Uffizi
See A–Z, Palazzo degli Uffizi

Galleria dello Spedale degli Innocenti
See A–Z, Spedale degli Innocenti

Raccolta di Arte Moderna "A. della Ragione"
Piazza Signoria 5
Open: Mon., Wed.–Sat. 9 a.m.–2 p.m.; Sun., public holidays
9 a.m.–1 p.m.
Closed: Tues.

Getting to Florence

It is a long way from Britain or northern Europe to Florence. Motorists will be well advised, therefore, to use motorways and main trunk roads as far as possible.

By car

Tolls are payable on the Italian motorways (autostrade). The tickets for each section should be preserved, since they must be given up when leaving the motorway.

Motorways

Motorists should carry their driving licence and car registration document. An international insurance certificate ("green card") is not obligatory but is advisable. The car should have a nationality plate, and a warning triangle must be carried.

Documents, etc.

Although there are several ways of getting to Italy, entry will most probably be by way of France or Switzerland. The major passes, which are closed in winter, are served by road or rail tunnels. the distance to Florence from the Channel ports is approximately 850–890 miles (1370–1430 km), requiring one or two night stops. Car-sleeper services operate during the summer from Boulogne, Brussels or Paris to Milan.

Roads to Florence

France–Italy, open 24 hours. Mont Blanc Tunnel: Chamonix–Aosta; Fréjus Tunnel: Chambéry–Turin.
Switzerland–Italy. The major frontier crossings between Switzerland and Italy, open 24 hours a day, are:

Frontier crossings

St Bernard (road tunnel): Lausanne–Aosta (the pass is usually closed from October to June); Simplon Pass (the pass is occasionally closed during the winter; alternative rail tunnel available): Brig–(rail tunnel NOT 24 hour service) Milan; Chiasso: Lugano–Como–Milan; Castasegna/Chiavenna (Maloja Pass): St Moritiz–Milan.

Austria–Italy. The following frontier crossings between Austria and Italy are open 24 hours a day.

Brenner Pass: Innsbruck–Bolzano; Résia (Reschen) Pass: Landeck–Merano–Bolzano; Arnbach/Prato alla Drave: Lienz–Dobbiaco–Cortina; Tarvisio: Villach–Udine–Venice.

There are numerous package tours by coach, either going direct to Florence or including Florence in a longer circuit. For information apply to any travel agent.
There are also various coach services between Britain or northern Europe and Florence.

By bus

Practical Information

By air

Florence does not have its own airport, but it can be reached by taking a scheduled flight from London to Pisa or Milan (daily) or Manchester to Milan (weekly) and then taking an Alitalia flight to Pisa's Galileo Galilei airport which is 53 miles (85 km) from Florence. Trains and buses run between Florence and Pisa, which has an hourly bus service from its airport to the main railway station in Florence.

Airlines

See Airlines, p. 138

By rail

The fastest route from London to Florence takes just over 25 hours, leaving London (Charing Cross) at 9 a.m., crossing the Channel by hovercraft and changing in Paris. The alternative route, with a through carriage from Hook of Holland to Florence, leaves London (Victoria) at 10 a.m. and takes just over 28 hours.

Rail services

See Rail services, p. 156

Hospitals (Ospedali)

Association of Florentine hospitals

Arcispedale di Santa Maria Nuova and association of Florentine hospitals
Central office tel. 2 77 41

The following hospitals are members of this association:

Santa Maria Nuova
Piazza S. Maria Nuova

Pediatrico Meyer (Children's hospital)
Via Luca Giordano 13

Generale di Careggi (General hospital)
Viale Morgagni

Villa Monna Tessa
Viale Pieraccini

Ponte Nuovo
Via delle Oblate

Policlinico Universitario
Viale Morgagni

Ospedale di Camerata
Via delle Piazzola 68, tel. 57 58 07

Ospedale di S. Giovanni di Dio
Borgognissanti 20, tel. 27 87 51

Ospedale S. Aloigi
Luzzi, Via dell'Uccellatoio-Pratolino, tel. 40 93 55

Ospedali Riuniti di San Antonino L. Campolmi e Camerata
Via della Piazzola 68, tel. 57 58 07

Istituto Ortopedico Toscano "Piero Palagi"   Orthopaedic hospital
Viale Michelangelo 41, tel. 68 13 811

Ospedale Oftalmico Fiorentino   Eye hospital
Via Massaccio 213, tel. 57 84 44

Ospedale "G. Banti e Salviatino"   Children's hospital
Via Lungo l'Affrico 276, tel. 60 20 21

Sun. and public holidays, tel. 47 78 91   Medical emergency service

tel. 21 22 22   Accidents

Hotels (Alberghi)

Hotels are officially classified into five categories (luxury, I, II,   Categories
III and IV) and pensions into three.

Tariffs vary considerably according to season. The rates given   Tariffs
in the following table (in lire) are based on information given
in the Italian State Tourist Office's list of hotels, "Alberghi
d'Italia". Increases are to be expected. Hotel bills should be
kept in case of enquiry by government inspectors into possible
tax evasion.

Category	Single room Rate for 1 person	Double room Rate for 2 persons
Hotels		
L	20,000–120,000	30,000–160,000
I	12,000– 60,000	18,000–120,000
II	8,500– 35,000	15,000– 55,000
III	6,000– 25,000	7,000– 35,000
IV	4,500– 18,000	6,000– 28,000
Pensions		
PI	5,000– 25,000	13,000– 33,000
PII	5,000– 18,000	7,000– 28,000
PIII	4,000– 12,000	5,000– 25,000

* Excelsior Italie, Piazza Ognissanti 3, L, 348 b.
* Villa Medici, Via il Prato 42, L, 193 b., SP
* Savoy, Piazza della Rupubblica 7, L, 173 b.
Grand Hotel Baglioni, Piazza Unità Italiana 6, I, 340 b.
Michelangelo, Viale Fratelli Rosselli 4, I, 253 b.
Jolly Carlton, Piazza Vittorio Veneto 4A, I, 249 b., SP
Anglo-American, Via Garibaldi 9, I, 202 b.
Grand Hotel Minerva, Piazza Santa Maria Novella 16, I, 199 b.,
SP
Plaza e Lucchesi, Lungarno della Zecca Vecchia 38, I, 191 b.
Croce di Malta, Via della Scala 7, I, 188 b., SP
Crest Hotel, Viale Europa 205, I, 184 b., SP
Londra, Via Iacopo da Diacceto 16, I, 184 b.
Grand Hotel Majestic, Via del Melarancio 1, I, 184 b.
Astoria Etap, Via del Giglio 9, I, 163 b.
De la Ville, Piazza Antinori 1, I, 128 b.
Kraft, Via Solferino, 2, I, 124 b., SP
Grandhotel Villa Cora, Viale Machiavelli 18, I, 97 b., SP
Park Palace, Piazzale Galileo 5, I, 52 b., SP
Principe, Lungarno Vespucci 34, I, 38 b.

Lungarno, Borgo San Jacopo 14, I, 138 b.
Augustus & Dei Congressi, Vicolo dell'Oro 5, I, 134 b.
Mediterraneo, Lungarno del Tempio 44, II, 668 b.
Residence Firenze Nova, Via Panchiatichi 51, II, 244 b.
Monginevro, Via di Novoli 59, II, 224 b.
Adriatico, Via Maso Finiguerra 9, II, 204 b.
Ambasciatori, Via Alamanni 3, II, 183 b.
Cavour, Via del Proconsolo 3, II, 171 b.
Mirage, Via Baracca 231, II, 164 b.
Columbus, Lungarno C. Colombo 22-A, II, 156 b.
Helvetia Bristol, Via de' Pescioni 2, II, 153 b.
Concorde, Viale L. Gori 10, II, 146 b.
Milano Terminus, Via Cerretani 10, II, 146 b.
Corona d'Italia, Via Nazionale 14, II, 149 b.
Capitol, Viale Amendola 34, II, 141 b.
Berchielli, Lungarno Acciaiuoli 14, II, 134 b.
Continental, Lungarno Acciaiuoli 2, II, 124 b.
Bonciani, Via Panzani 17, II, 114 b.
Auto Hotel Park, Via Valdegola 1, III, 198 b.
Nuovo Atlantico, Via Nazionale 10, III, 174 b.
Fleming, Viale Guidoni 87, III, 172 b.; and many more

Daytime hotels (Alberghi Diurni)

Diurno Stazione Santa Maria Novella, Piazza S.M. Novella, tel. 21 52 88
Diurno Bar Alfieri, Via Pepi 28, tel. 28 34 62

In these hotels rooms can be rented by the hour in order to wash, take a bath or get a shave and a haircut.

Insurance

Car Insurance

It is very desirable to have an international insurance certificate ("Green card"), although this is not a legal requirement for citizens of EEC countries. It is important to have fully comprehensive cover, and it is desirable to take out short-term insurance against legal costs if these are not already covered. Italian insurance companies tend to be slow in settling claims.

Health insurance

British visitors to Italy, like other EEC citizens, are entitled to receive health care on the same basis as Italians (including free medical treatment, etc.); they should apply to their local social security office, well before their date of departure, for a certificate of entitlement (form E111). Fuller cover can be obtained by taking out insurance against medical expenses; and non-EEC citizens will, of course, be well advised to take out appropriate insurance cover.

Baggage insurance

In view of the risk of theft it is desirable to have adequate insurance against loss of, or damage to, baggage.

Libraries (Biblioteche)

Biblioteca dell'Accademia della Crusca
Villa Medicea di Castello or Piazza dei Giudici, 1
open 9 a.m.–1 p.m., 3.30–7 p.m.; closed Sat.

Biblioteca dell'Accademia dei Georgofili
Loggiato degli Uffizi
open 3.30–7 p.m.; closed in August

Biblioteca e Archivio Comunale
Via S. Egidio 21
open 8.30 a.m.–1 p.m.

Biblioteca della Facoltà di Lettere e Filisofia
Piazza Brunelleschi
open Mon.–Fri. 8.30 a.m.–7.30 p.m.; Sat. 8.30 a.m.–1 p.m.

Biblioteca del Gabinetto Vieusseux
Palazzo Strozzi or Via Maggio 42
open Mon.–Fri. 9 a.m.–1 p.m., 3–5 p.m.; Sat. 9 a.m.–1 p.m.

Biblioteca dell'Istituto Britannico
Lungarno Guicciardini 9
open 10 a.m.–12.30, 4–6.30 p.m.; closed Sat.

Biblioteca e Archivio del Risorgimento
Via S. Egidio 21
open 9–7 p.m.; closed Sat.

Biblioteca dell'Istituto Francese
Piazza Ognissanti 2
open 10 a.m.–12.30, 3–7 p.m.

Biblioteca dell'Istituto di Studi sul Rinascimento
Palazzo Strozzi
open 9 a.m.–12.30, 3.30–6.30 p.m.; Sat. 9 a.m.–12.30

Biblioteca dell'Istituto Tedesco di Storia del'Arte
Via Giusti 44
open 9 a.m.–12.30, 3–10 p.m.; closed Sat.

Biblioteca Marucelliana
Via Cavour 43
open Mon.–Fri. 9 a.m.–1 p.m., 3–7.30 p.m.
(January–June 3–9 p.m.); Sat. 9 a.m.–1 p.m.

Biblioteca Mediceo-Laurenziana
See A–Z, San Lorenzo
open 9 a.m.–2 p.m.; Sat. 8 a.m.–1 p.m.

Biblioteca Nazionale Centrale
See A–Z, Biblioteca Nazionale Centrale

Biblioteca Riccardiana e Moreniana
Via Ginorei 10
open 8 a.m.–2 p.m.; Sat. 8 a.m.–1 p.m.

Lost property offices (Servizi oggetti rinvenuti)

Ufficio Oggetti smarriti
Lungarno delle Grazie 22, tel. 36 79 43

Municipal lost property
office

Ufficio Oggetti rinvenuti (Lost property office)
Santa Maria Novella Railway Station
Central office tel. 27 67, ext. 2190

Markets (Mercati)

Fruit and vegetable markets	The fruit and vegetable markets are open daily in the mornings only. Particularly worth seeing: Mercato Centrale (Near San Lorenzo) Mercato Sant'Embrogio, Piazza Ghiberti
Weekly market	The weekly market on Tuesdays in the Parco delle Cascine sells mainly clothing in addition to general goods.
Flea market	Via Pietrapiana Piaza Ghiberti, Piazza dei Ciompi (also antiques) (Both permanent markets)
Straw market	Loggia del Mercato Nuovo Via Porta Rossa/Via Calzaiuoli Open: Mon.–Fri.; closed Sat. Craftwork in straw, ceramics, leather and knitware. Market of San Lorenzo Piazza San Lorenzo Open Mon.–Fri.; closed Sat.

Fruit and vegetable markets – part of daily life

Souvenirs and pictures on sale in the arcades of the Palazzo degli Uffizi

Motoring

The main types of road are:
Motorways (autostrade) numbered A ... Tolls are payable.
State highways (strade statali) numbered SS ... Many of them
have names (Via Aurelia, Via Emilia, etc.), which are often
better known than their numbers.
Provincial highways (strade di grande comunicazione) which
have no numbers.
Secondary roads (strade secondarie) for local traffic.

The road system

Within built-up areas the speed limit is 31 m.p.h. (50 km p.h.).
Outside built-up areas the limits vary according to cylinder
capacity:

Speed limits

Ordinary roads	Motorways		Capacity
50 m.p.h. (80 km p.h.)	56 m.p.h. (90 km p.h.)		up to 600 cc
56 m.p.h. (90 km p.h.)	68 m.p.h. (110 km p.h.)		up to 900 cc
62 m.p.h. (100 km p.h.)	81 m.p.h. (130 km p.h.)		up to 1300 cc
68 m.p.h. (110 km p.h.)	87 m.p.h. (140 km p.h.)		over 1300 cc

The wearing of safety belts is strongly recommended.

Safety belts

All motorists must carry a warning triangle and it is
recommended that cars are equipped with a spare set of light
bulbs.

Compulsory equipment

149

Practical Information

Priority

Traffic on main roads has priority where the road is marked with the priority sign (a square with a corner pointing downwards, coloured white with a red border or yellow with a black and white border).

Mountain roads

On mountain roads traffic going up has priority.

Change of lane

Any change of lane (for overtaking or any other purpose) must be signalled with the direction indicator, as must an intention to stop by the roadside.

Overtaking

Outside built-up areas the horn must be sounded before overtaking. It must also be sounded before intersections, side roads, blind bends and other hazards. After dark flashing headlights should be used for the same purpose.

Prohibition on use of horn

In towns the use of horns is frequently prohibited, either by an appropriate road sign (a horn with a stroke through it) or by the legend "Zona di silenzio".

Lights

On well-lit roads sidelights only may be used (except in tunnels and galleries where dipped headlights must be used at all times).

Zebra crossings

Pedestrians have absolute priority on zebra crossings.

Traffic police

The directions of the traffic police (polizia stradale) should be strictly observed. Fines for traffic offences are high.

Petrol

A package of petrol coupons giving a saving on the pump price can be purchased from the AA or at main ports and border crossings.
It is forbidden to carry petrol in cans in a vehicle.

Drinking and driving

There are heavy penalties for driving under the influence of alcohol.

Accidents

In the event of an accident make sure that you have all the necessary particulars and supporting evidence (statements by witnesses, sketches, photographs, etc.). If the accident involves personal injury it must be reported to the police. You should notify your own insurance company as soon as possible, and if you are responsible or partly responsible for the accident you should also inform the Italian insurance company or bureau whose address is given on your green card. This agency will give advice and supply the name of a lawyer should the foreign driver be subject to penal proceedings. – If your car is a total write-off the Italian customs authorities must be informed at once, since otherwise you might be required to pay the full import duty on the vehicle.

Breakdown assistance

In case of breakdown on any Italian road just dial 116 at the nearest telephone box. Tell the operator where you are, registration number and type of car and the nearest ACI office will be informed for immediate assistance.

Automobile Club

Automobile Club d'Italia (ACI)
Viale Amendola 36, tel. 2 78 41

Puncture repair

Look for the sign "Riparazione gomme".

Look for "Officina".

Anywhere in Italy dial 113.

For reports on road conditions, etc. in Tuscany dial 194.

See Car hire, p. 140

Museums

Casa Buonarotti (Michelangelo Museum)
See A–Z, Casa Buonarroti

Casa e Museo di Dante (Dante Museum)
See A–Z, Casa di Dante

Castagno Museum
See A–Z, Cenacolo di Sant'Apollonio

Conservatore Musicale Luigi Cherubini
See A–Z, Conservatorio Musicale Luigi Cherubini

Museo dell'Antica Casa Fiorentina (Museo Davanzati)
See A–Z, Pallazzo Davanzati

Museo di Antropologia ed Etnologia
(Museum of Mankind)
See A–Z, Pallazo Nonfinito

Museo Archeologico Centrale dell'Etruria
See A–Z, Museo Archeologico Centrale dell'Etruria

Museo degli Argenti
See A–Z, Pallazzo Pitti

Museo Bardini e Galleria Corsi
See A–Z, Museo Bardini

Museo del Bigallo
See A–Z, Monastero del Bigallo

Museo delle Carrozze (Coach Museum)
See A–Z, Palazzo Pitti

Museo della Fondazione Horne
See A–Z, Museo della Fondazione Horne

Museo di Geologia e Paleontologia dell'Università
Via La Pira 4
Open Mon. 2–5.30 p.m., Thurs, Sat. 10 a.m.–1 p.m.

Museo Mediceo (Medici Museum)
See A–Z, Palazzo Medici Riccardi

Museo di Mineralogia e Litologia dell'Università
Via La Pira 4
Open 9 a.m.–noon; closed Sun., public holidays

Practical Information

Museo Nazionale del Bargello
See A–Z, Palazzo Bargello

Museo dell'Opera del Duomo (Museo di Santa Maria del Fiore)
See A–Z, Museo dell'Opera del Duomo

Museo dell'Opera di Santa Croce
See A–Z, Santa Croce

Museo e Orto Botanico
See A–Z, Orto Botanico

Museo delle Porcellane
See A–Z, Giardino di Boboli

Museo di Preistoria
Via S. Egidio 21
Open 9.30 a.m.–12.30; closed Mon.

Museo di San Marco
See A–Z, San Marco

Museo Stibbert
See A–Z, Museo Stibbert

Museo (e Istituto) di Storia della Scienza
(History of Science)
See A–Z, Palazzo Castellani

Museo Storico Topografico "Firenze com'era"
See A–Z, Museo Storico Topografico

Museo Zoologico "La Specoloa"
See A–Z, Museo Zoologico

Opificio e Museo delle Pietre Dure
(Mosaic Museum)
See A–Z, Opificio e Museo delle Pietre Dure

Music

Opera	Teatro Comunale Corso Italia 16
	Teatro della Pergola Via della Pergola 12
Concerts	Sala Bianca, Palazzo Pitti
	Sala del Conservatorio di Musica, Piazza Belle Arti 2
Maggio Musicale Fiorentino	This famous music festival lasts throughout May and June and includes performances by the world's great artists.
Ballet	In summer there are ballet performances in the Palazzo Pitti and the Giardino di Boboli (see A–Z).

Opening times

Summer 9 a.m.–12.30, 4–8 p.m.
Closed Sat. afternoon.   Shops

Winter 9 a.m.–12.30, 3.30–7.30 p.m.
Closed Mon. morning.

Summer Mon.–Fri. 8.30 a.m.–12.30, 4–8 p.m.   Chemists
Winter Mon.–Fri. 8.30 a.m.–12.30, 3.30–7.30 p.m.

Open 8.30 a.m.–1 p.m.   Banks

Open 8.15 a.m.–2 p.m.   Post offices

Petrol stations are usually closed between 12.30 and 3.30 p.m.   Petrol stations
and from 8 p.m. (in winter usually 7 p.m.).

The public museums are generally open from 9 or 10 a.m. to 1   Museums
or 2 p.m. and from 2 or 3 p.m. to 5 or 6 p.m., rarely to 7 p.m.; a
few remain open throughout the day, without a lunch break. In
winter (when the museums are for the most part inadequately
heated) the opening hours are usually shorter, but during the
more restricted hours they often remain open without a break
at lunchtime.
All museums are closed on Sunday afternoons and statutory
public holidays; most of them are also closed on Mondays, or
sometimes Fridays. On various other days in the year the state
museums are open only in the mornings and other museums are
closed all day. In addition there are often closures as a result of
staff shortages, strikes, renovation, etc. It is advisable,
therefore, before visiting a museum, to check that it will be
open.

The larger churches are usually open until noon and for the   Churches
most part also from 4 or 5 p.m. until dusk; some of the major
churches are open all day. It is possible to see the interior of a
church during a service if care is taken to avoid disturbing the
worshippers. Visitors should always be suitably dressed,
avoiding short-sleeved dresses or blouses, mini-skirts, shorts,
short-sleeved shirts, etc. If inappropriately dressed they may be
refused admittace. Cover-up garments can be hired at many
church entrances.

Pets

Dogs must wear muzzles and be kept on a leash.

In view of the stringent regulations regarding the prevention of
rabies you are strongly advised not to attempt to take pets in or
out of the UK.

Police

Questura	Police headquarters, Via Zara 2, tel. 49 77
Carabinieri	Borgognissanti 48, tel. 21 21 21
Vigili urbani	Municipal police, Piazzale della Porta al Prato 6, tel. 49 66 46
Polizia stradale	Traffic police, tel. 57 77 77

Postal services (Posta)

Postal rates	Letters within Italy and to EEC countries up to 400 lire. Postcards up to 200 lire. Express letters up to 1200 lire.
Letter boxes	In Italy letter boxes are painted red.
Post offices	Post offices are usually only open from 8.15 a.m. to 2 p.m. but the main post office in the Piazza Repubblica is also open in the afternoon and evening for special services.
Stamps	Stamps can be bought at post offices, at tobacconists (indicated by a large T above the door) and from stamp machines.

Public holidays

1 January (New Year's Day); 25 April (Liberation Day, 1945).

Easter Monday; 1 May (Labour Day).

15 August (Assumption: a family celebration, the high point of the Italian summer holiday migration).

1 November (All Saints); 8 December (Immaculate Conception).

25 and 26 December (Christmas).

Public transport

Buses	Buses are the only form of public transport in Florence.
	For information from ATAF, the public transport headquarters call 21 23 01.
	Since most buses have automatic ticket machines it is necessary to carry plenty of small change. The flat-rate is 200 lire (as of 1.1.1981). Most sightseeing can be done on foot, however, since the distances between the sights of Florence are not very great.

Radio

Information on overseas radio transmissions may be obtained from BBC External Services, P.O. Box 76, Bush House, London WC2B 4PH.

Programmes in English

Railway stations

The main railway station for national and international passenger traffic is:
Stazione Centrale Santa Maria Novella

tel. 27 87 85 (8 a.m.–12.30,. 3.30–7 p.m.).

Information

(Ufficio Oggetti Rinvenuti): head office tel. 27 67

Lost property

tel. 21 22 96

Railway police

Sleeper and couchette reservations can only be made in the ticket offices at the station.

Reservations

Available in the main station.

Accommodation service

Florence, main railway station

Rail services

Ferrovie dello Stato (FS)	The Italian railway system has a total length of 10,000 miles (16,000 km). Most of it is run by the Italian State Railways (Ferrovie dello Stato – FS).

Information about rail services, and the concessionary fares available, can be obtained from the Italian State Tourist Office or from Italian State Railways offices abroad: |
| United Kingdon | 10 Charles II Street, London SW1; tel. (01) 434 3844 |
| United States of America | 765 Route 83, Suite 105, Chicago, Ill.
5670 Wilshire Boulevard, Los Angeles, Cal.
668 Fifth Avenue, New York, NY. |
| Canada | 2055 Peel Street, Suite 102, Montreal.
111 Richmond Street West, Suite 419, Toronto. |
| In Florence | Stazione Centrale Santa Maria Novella, tel.: 27 87 85 |
| Children | Children accompanied by an adult travel free up to the age of 4; between 4 and 14 they pay half fare. |

Restaurants (Ristorante)

A selection of recommended restaurants:
*Sabatini, Via de Panzani 41
Doney, Via Tornabuoni 10
Olivero, Via delle Terme 51r
Paoli, Via de' Tavolini 12r
Al Campidoglio, Via del Campidoglio 8r
Otello, Via Orti Orticellari 28r
Giannino in San Lorenzo, Via Borso San Lorenzo 37r
Buca Lapi, Via del Trebbio 1r
La Loggia, Piazzale Michelangelo 1

Warning Keep your restaurant bill in case of enquiry by inspectors investigating tax evasion.

Shopping

The streets and alleys in the Centro Storico (historical centre) are where you will find the finest shops and most elegant fashion houses, offering a broad range of shoes, bags, knitwear, clothing, jewellery and lingerie.

Opening times

9 a.m.–12.30, 3.30–7.30 p.m.
In the summer shops open and close half an hour later; shops are closed on Saturday afternoon in the summer and on Monday morning in the winter. Foodshops are closed on Wednesday afternoon.

Department store chains have only a few shops in Florence:

Via dello Statuto 19	UPIM
Piazza della Repubblica	
Via Gioberti	
Viale Talenti	
Via Panzani 31	STANDA
Via Pietrapiana 42/44	
Piazza Dalmazia 14	

Shopping streets

Ponte Vecchio	Goldsmiths, silversmiths
Piazza Santa Croce, Piazza San Lorenzo	Leather goods
Piazza della Repubblica, Via Calzaiuoli, Via Tornabuoni	Shoes
Via Calzaiuoli, Via Tornabuoni	Clothing, lingerie
In the quarter Santa Croce	Books
See Markets, p. 148	Markets

Florence also has its mobile bookshops

Sightseeing

Information on organised sightseeing tours can be obtained from the Italian State Tourist Offices (see Tourist Information, p. 159).

Authorised guides

For an individual sightseeing tour a guide can be hired through "Ufficio Guide Turistiche", Viale Gramsci, 9a, tel. 67 91 88.

Sports facilities

Stadium

Stadio Comunale
Viale Manfredo Fanti
Stadium (55,000 seats), swimming pool

Race-courses

Galoppo Ippodromo del Visarno
Trotto Ippodromo delle Muline Cascine, see A–Z, Cascine

Golf

Golf dell'Ugolino
Grassina, Strada Chiatigiana 3 (7·5 miles – 12 km out of Florence)

Tennis

Circolo del Tennis, Cascine, Viale Visarno 1

Swimming pools

Open air pools

Piscina Bellariva
Lungarno Colombo

Piscina Costoli
Viale Paoli

Piscina Pavoniere
Viale degli Olmi

Taxis

Radio taxis

Tel. 43 90 or 47 98

Taxi ranks

Taxi ranks are listed, together with their telephone numbers and a map, in the front of the classified telephone directory (Pagine Gialle).

Telephone

International dialling code from Florence

To the United Kingdom: 00 04
(Direct dialling not available to the United States and Canada.)

International dialling code to Florence

From the United Kingdom: 010 39 55
From the United States: 011 39 55
From Canada: 011 39 55

In dialling an international call the initial zero of the local dialling code should be omitted.

Most bars have public telephones (indicated by a yellow disc above the entrance to the box), operated by tokens (*gettoni*), from which local calls can be dialled. If the yellow disc bears the legend "teleselezione" or "interurbana" international calls can be dialled – though for this purpose you must provide yourself with an adequate supply of tokens. The present cost of a *gettone* is 100 lire.

Public telephones

There are also public telephones in post offices and in the offices of the SIP (the state telephone corporation).

Post offices

Theatres

Teatro Verdi (light entertainment)
Via Ghibellina 99

Teatro dell'Oriuolo (drama)
Via dell'Oriuolo 31

Palazzo dei Congressi
Viale Filippo Strozzi
Cultural events are staged in the summer for tourists in the Palazzo dei Congressi.

Special shows for tourists

See Music, p. 152

Music Theatre

Time

Italy observes Central European Time (one hour ahead of Greenwich Mean Time; six hours ahead of New York time). From the end of March to the end of September summer time (two hours ahead of GMT; seven hours ahead of New York time) is in force.

Tipping (Mancia)

A good general rule is to tip for a special service although everyone is pleased to have his or her services recognised in this way.

Tourist information

The first place to go for information when you are planning a trip to Florence is the Italian State Tourist Office.

1 Princes Street, London W1A 7RA;
tel. 01–408 1254

United Kingdom

500 North Michigan Avenue, Chicago, IL 60611;
tel. (312) 644 0990–1
630 Fifth Avenue, Suite 1565, New York, NY 10111;
tel. (212) 245 4822–4
360 Post Street, Suite 801, San Francisco, CA 94108;
tel. (415) 392 6206–7

United States of America

Practical Information

Canada

c/o Alitalia, 85 Richmond Street, Toronto;
tel. (416) 36–31–348

In Florence

Ufficio Informazioni Turistiche dell'Ente Provinciale per il
Turismo
Via A-Manzoni 16, tel. 67 88 41–5

Ufficio Informazioni Turistiche dell'Azienda Autonoma di
Turismo
Via Tornabuoni 15, tel. 216 544/5

Ufficio Informazioni Turistiche
in the main station

Travel agencies (Uffici di viaggio)

Travel agencies which also offer excursions (see Excursions,
p. 142:

Arno Travel Service
Piazza Ottaviani 7r, tel. 29 52 51

Chiariva
Via Vacchereccia 26r, tel. 21 19 68

C.I.T.
Via Cerretani 57r, tel. 29 43 06
Piazza Stazione 51r, tel. 28 41 45

Globus Travel Service
Piazza S. Trinità 2r, tel 21 49 92

Travel documents

Passport

British and US citizens require only a passport (or the simpler
British visitor's passport). This applies also to citizens of
Canada, Ireland and many other countries.

If you lose your passport a substitute document can be issued
by the British, US, Canadian, etc. consulate. It is a good idea to
photocopy or note down the main particulars (number, date,
etc.) of your passport, so that in case of loss you can give the
necessary details to the police.

Driving licence, etc.

British, US and other national driving licences are valid in Italy,
but must be accompanied by an Italian translation (obtainable
free of charge from the AA). Motorists should also take the
registration document of their car.

Green card

See Insurance, p. 146.

Nationality plate

Foreign cars must display the oval nationality plate.

Youth hostel

Ostello della Gioventù
Viale Righi 2/4, tel. 60 03 15; Bus: 17 red